Essential Questions in EU Law

To the new student of EU law, deciding what questions to ask on the subject is as much of a challenge as answering them. This introduction's distinctive Q & A format immediately directs the student to the questions he or she should be asking. Concise and clearly structured, it guides students through the different layers of the European Union from the law establishing it, through how its institutions work and on to its operation on the international stage. It also provides a clear explanation of the substantive law of the EU and the working of the internal market. Each chapter takes a cornerstone of EU law, sets the scene with a short introductory overview and then tackles its key questions. Providing enough detail to give a solid foundation to this complex subject without losing the student with excessive detail, it is an essential first port-of-call for study of the subject.

AUGUST REINISCH is Professor of International and European Law at the University of Vienna and Adjunct Professor at the Bologna Center of The Paul H. Nitze School of Advanced International Studies of Johns Hopkins University.

Essential Questions in
EU Law

AUGUST REINISCH

CAMBRIDGE
UNIVERSITY PRESS

CAMBRIDGE UNIVERSITY PRESS
Cambridge, New York, Melbourne, Madrid, Cape Town, Singapore,
São Paulo, Delhi

Cambridge University Press
The Edinburgh Building, Cambridge CB2 8RU, UK

Published in the United States of America by Cambridge University Press,
New York

www.cambridge.org
Information on this title: www.cambridge.org/9780521730280

© August Reinisch 2009

First published 2009

Printed in the United Kingdom at the University Press, Cambridge

A catalogue record for this publication is available from the British Library

ISBN 978-0-521-51394-4 hardback
ISBN 978-0-521-73028-0 paperback

Contents

Abbreviations

ACP	African, Caribbean and Pacific
ALDE	Alliance of Liberals and Democrats for Europe
CAP	Common Agricultural Policy
CCP	Common Commercial Policy
CFI	Court of First Instance
CFSP	Common Foreign and Security Policy
CIS	Commonwealth of Independent States
CMLR	Common Market Law Reports
COREPER	Permanent Representatives Committee
CSFR	Czech and Slovak Federal Republic
CT	(draft) Constitution Treaty
DG	Directorate-General
ECHR	European Convention on Human Rights
ECtHR	European Court of Human Rights
ECJ	European Court of Justice
ECOFIN	Council for Economic and Financial Affairs
ECR	European Court Reports
ECSC	European Coal and Steel Community
EEA	European Economic Area
EEC	European Economic Community
EESC	European Economic and Social Committee
EFTA	European Free Trade Agreement
EHRR	European Human Rights Reports
EMU	European Monetary Union
EP	European Parliament
EPC	European Political Cooperation
EPP-ED	Group of the European People's Party (Christian Democrats) and European Democrats

ERTA	European Road Transport Agreement
ESDP	European Security and Defence Policy
EURATOM	European Atomic Energy Community
GATS	General Agreement on Trade in Services
GATT	General Agreement on Tariffs and Trade
GNP	Gross national product
GUE/NGL	Confederal Group of the European United Left/ Nordic Green Left
ILO	International Labour Organization
IND/DEM	Independence/Democracy Group in the European Parliament
JHA	Cooperation in Justice and Home Affairs
MEP	Member of European Parliament
NATO	North Atlantic Treaty Organization
OECD	Organization for Economic Cooperation and Development
OEEC	Organization for European Economic Cooperation
OJ	Official Journal
PES	Group of the Party of European Socialists
PJCC	Police and Judicial Cooperation in Criminal Matters
QMV	Qualified majority voting
SEA	Single European Act
TEC	Treaty on the European Community
TEU	Treaty on European Union
TRIPs	Agreement on Trade Related Intellectual Property Rights
UEN	Union for Europe of the Nations Group
UNCTAD	United Nations Conference on Trade and Development
VAT	Value added tax
Les Verts	Group of the Greens/European Free Alliance
WEU	Western European Union
WLR	Weekly Law Reports
WTO	World Trade Organization

Preface

This little book owes its existence to a number of factors, most importantly the persistent requests of my students both at the Bologna Center of Johns Hopkins University and at Bocconi University in Milan for a simple and readable, and preferably short, introduction to the law of the European Union. It was, and remains, a particular challenge to teach EU/EC law in institutions with mostly economics and political science students, who are not always wholly enthusiastic about learning the law. That made me realise that there is a lack of available academic resources for this particular purpose. Of course, there are the excellent treatises by Craig and De Burca on *EU Law*, now already in its fourth edition (2008), and the *European Union Law* by Chalmers, Hadjiemmanuil, Monti and Tomkins (2006), as well as a number of other first-rate law books – needless to say, not always a light fare even for law students. The students at my home law school at the University of Vienna equally demanded access to learning the law in a most time-efficient manner.

Being brief on EU law is, of course, like squaring the circle, with the additional, hermeneutic complication that it is almost impossible to understand anything fully without first understanding everything, at least a little. This book has been written against all these odds. It aims at explaining the most important institutional aspects of the European Union, the interplay of its main bodies in the process of European legislation, the control of legality exercised by the two Community Courts, the importance of fundamental rights in this context and the role of the EU as an international actor. It equally tries to familiarise the reader with the most important aspects of so-called substantive Community law, that is, the law of the four freedoms, in particular, the free movement of goods in the internal market and the freedom rights of EU citizens as workers, self-employed and family members. In addition, a number of other Community policies, such as the Common Agricultural Policy (CAP) together with matters of environmental and consumer protection are outlined, while a more detailed inquiry is made into European competition law.

In all these areas, the main principles stemming from the 1992 Treaty on European Union (TEU) as well as from the 1957 Treaty Establishing the European Community (TEC), both in their amended and currently valid forms, as they have been published in consolidated versions after the Nice Treaty amendments 2002, are outlined and discussed together with the major rules contained in EU legislation. Where appropriate, provisions of the Draft Constitution Treaty and the Lisbon Reform Treaty are discussed as well, although it appears unlikely that the changes envisaged therein will be adopted in the near future. When discussing the law, particular emphasis is laid on the case law of the European Court of Justice (ECJ) and its Court of First Instance (CFI), which should make the sometimes rather tedious rules and principles livelier and more accessible.

The specific Questions and Answers format was deliberately chosen in order to move away from the usual textbook structure and provide easy access to the core issues of EU law. Instead of lengthy footnotes or endnotes and ample indices and tables of cases, instruments, etc., a light system of cross-references will guide the users through this book, remind them of content they have already read in earlier chapters, or alert them to further explanations in subsequent chapters. Additionally, bold print is used where necessary in order to indicate the most important terms and concepts used in EU law.

A final disclaimer is warranted: do not use this little book as a substitute for further and more detailed study of EU law! It is intended only to provide a first and general introduction into a fascinating and ever growing body of law and should encourage the reader to do so. If it does, it has been successful.

August Reinisch
Vienna, September 2008

1 History of European integration

For centuries, the history of the small continent, or quasi-continent, of Europe has been a history of war and peace, where rival political entities, predominantly in the form of **nation-states**, have tried to dominate each other. The terrible twentieth-century experience of two World Wars, fought mainly on European territory, provided the necessary impetus to seek alternative ways of political survival, co-existence, or even cooperation. In its historic context, European integration must be understood as an attempt primarily motivated by the desire to secure peace and stability through establishing appropriate institutions. The institutions created in post-war Europe were based on ideas, partly dating back to the Middle Ages. However, it was the situation after 1945 which made it possible to think about actually setting up new structures which would make war in Europe, if not impossible, then at least less likely. The creation of a **European Coal and Steel Community** (ECSC) in 1951, by which two strategically important industry sectors of rival nations like France and Germany were pooled, was such an important and highly pragmatic first step. It was soon followed by the establishment of two further organisations, the **European Economic Community** (EEC) and the **European Atomic Energy Community** (EURATOM) in 1957, which were designed as open regional organisations with a long-term goal of a yet undefined European unity.

Until today the process of European integration has been

characterised by a constant tension between the maintenance of individual Member State power and further integration, leading to 'an ever closer union among the peoples of Europe', as promised in the opening lines of the 1957 Treaty of Rome's preamble.

This introductory chapter is intended to provide an overview of European integration. In the course of this process, the three initially rather specialised, supranational organisations, the ECSC, the EEC and EURATOM, developed into a single comprehensive and highly integrated entity called the European Union (EU).

? 1.1 Does the history of ideas provide antecedents for European integration?

European political philosophy provides numerous examples of political concepts transgressing the nation-state. Some commentators have referred back as far as Pierre Dubois, the late medieval Frenchman, who suggested an assembly of delegates presided over by the French king in order to realise the old dream of the crusaders to recapture the Holy Land (*De recuperatione terrae sanctae*, 1306). The proposal by Dubois' contemporary, the Italian poet Dante Alighieri, demonstrates that the history of ideas has always been highly influenced by day-to-day politics. As a staunch supporter of the Ghibbelines and opponent of the Guelfs who supported the Papacy, Dante preferred the leadership of the (German) Holy Roman Emperor (*Monarchia*, 1308 or later).

Quite concrete and surprisingly 'modern' suggestions were made: for instance, by William Penn, who proposed a 'European Union' with decision making on the basis of weighted voting (*An Essay Towards the Present and Future Peace of Europe*, 1693); or by the Abbé de Saint Pierre, who advocated a sophisticated institutional framework including elements such as unanimity and qualified majority voting ($\rightarrow$ *2.5*), and an internal dispute settlement mechanism (*Projet pour rendre la paix perpétuelle en Europe*, 1713). This principal purpose of guaranteeing a perpetual peace remained central to the plans of Jean Jacques Rousseau (*Extrait du projet de paix perpétuelle*, 1761) and Immanuel Kant (*Zum ewigen Frieden*, 1795).

In these early phases, however, European integration plans could hardly be separated from larger concepts such as world confederation and world government. It was only after the First World War that a specific regional integration concept for Europe was developed. Both the vision of the Pan-European Movement by Count Richard Nikolaus Coudenhove-Kalergi (*Das Pan-Europäische Manifest*, 1923) and the specific proposals by the French Foreign Minister, Aristide Briand, in 1929, which even led to a 'Study Group on European Union' set up by the League of Nations, proved to be utopian in the face of rising nationalism and fascism.

The Second World War, while destroying any hopes for Pan-Europa, at the same time demonstrated the necessity of European integration in order to avoid future wars. In his famous Zurich speech in 1946 Winston Churchill proposed a sort of 'United States of Europe'. The time was ripe to actually start thinking about how to bring about European integration.

? 1.2 Explain the philosophies underlying the concepts of federalism and functionalism in the context of European integration

There were essentially two rival concepts concerning the actual steps which were required in order to reach the common goal of European integration: federalism and functionalism.

On the one hand, the 'federalists', building on various political movements formed in (Western) Europe in the late 1940s, pursued a more 'radical' path with a view to forming a United States of Europe by designing a constitution for a federal Europe in which political union was a logical first step.

'Functionalists', on the other hand, took a more 'pragmatic' approach. Their leading advocates, the French politicians Robert Schuman and Jean Monnet, thought that integrating strategically important sectors of the economy, and thereby removing them from national control, would not only make military confrontation among the Members materially impossible, but also – in the long run – lead to further economic and other integration. Ultimately, as neo-functionalist theory stressed, the 'spill-over effect' of economic integration could even lead to political union (→ 1.8).

The **Schuman Plan**, presented in May 1950, used these ideas and proposed the merger of the French and German coal and steel industry by putting it under shared control and inviting other European nations to join.

1.3 Outline the early history of European supranational integration

European integration closely followed what the functionalists had expected. The Schuman Plan led to the 1951 Paris Treaty establishing the European Coal and Steel Community (ECSC) comprising France, Germany, Italy and the Benelux countries (Belgium, the Netherlands and Luxembourg). This treaty entered into force in July 1952 for a period of fifty years, and it set up the first truly **supranational** (→ 1.5) organisation with a 'High Authority', its main organ, having far-reaching powers in order to create a common market in coal and steel.

The ECSC was a useful blueprint for further economic

integration and in 1955 – after the unsuccessful attempts to set up a **European Defence Community** ($\rightarrow$ *1.8*) – the ECSC Member States at their conference in Messina decided to turn 'back to economics'. They entrusted the task of elaborating proposals for further integration to an expert committee, headed by the Belgian politician, Paul Henri Spaak. By March 1957, the ECSC founding states had convened to sign the **Treaties of Rome**, establishing a European Economic Community (EEC) and a European Atomic Energy Community (EURATOM), which both entered into force on 1 January 1958.

? 1.4 Which other post-war European organisations could have served as a framework for further integration?

European integration via the three Communities is embedded in the larger context of a number of 'European' international organisations founded after the Second World War.

Among the 'transatlantic' organisations, the **Organization for European Economic Cooperation (OEEC)**, founded in 1948, served primarily to administer the delivery of the United States Marshall Plan aid to Europe (European Recovery Program). In 1960, it was transformed into the **Organization for Economic Cooperation and Development (OECD)**.

The most important military – equally 'transatlantic' – organisation is the North Atlantic Treaty Organization (NATO) founded in 1949. Its European counterpart is the **Western European Union (WEU)**, which was established in 1954 and is based on the 1948 Brussels Treaty originally concluded between France, the United Kingdom and the Benelux countries. Today, the WEU is expected to become the defence arm of the EU.

Among the 'general political' organisations, the **Council** of Europe, founded in 1949, covers a broad variety of issues, excluding defence. Its weak decision-making procedures, however, have prevented it from gaining a role competing with the European Communities. Still, in the field of human rights, the Council of Europe successfully elaborated the 1950 European Convention on Human Rights (ECHR) as well as later protocols amending it. It also provided an institutional mechanism of supervision through the European Commission and the European Court of Human Rights (ECtHR). The rights and freedoms contained in the ECHR are considered to form part of Community law as expressions of general principles of law (→*6.2, 6.6*). They also feature prominently in the (non-binding) EU Charter of Fundamental Rights solemnly adopted at the Nice Conference in 2000 (→*6.15*).

? 1.5 Describe the characteristics of a supranational organisation

The term 'supranational' was first expressly used in the ECSC Treaty characterising the High Authority until this institution was merged with the Commission in the 1965 Merger Treaty (→ *2.1*), which in effect replaced the three distinct sets of Community institutions under the three legally separate Communities by a single set of institutions. There have been many attempts to define the notion of a 'supranational' – as opposed to a weaker 'international' or 'intergovernmental' – organisation. Since none of them is completely satisfactory, the prevailing view nowadays prefers to identify a number of characteristic elements, the combined existence of which should allow one to speak of a 'supranational' organisation.

These elements include, most importantly, majority voting in the decision-making institutions (→ *2.5, 2.6*) with the power to bind outvoted Members (→ *3.4*), a system of obligatory dispute settlement (→ *5.4*), the direct effect (→ *4.1, 4.4*) and supremacy (→ *4.10, 4.11*) of EC law in/over national law, and the existence of 'own resources' (→ *2.20*) of the organisation. All these elements will be explained in more detail in later sections of this book.

? 1.6 What was the widening vs. deepening debate about?

The widening vs. deepening debate concerns the question of whether enlargement or internal enhancement of the Communities/the Union should come first. With the geopolitical changes of 1989 this ceased to be an academic question, and instead became one of the central issues dominating the political debate from the 1990s to the present.

It was felt that widening may lead to a lowering of the speed of integration, while deepening could create a 'fortress Europe' locking out the Eastern half of the continent. The political choice made was to try to avoid both situations and, thus, to aim for both widening and deepening at the same time.

Attempts have been made to tackle the problem of losing common ground when opening the Union to more Members by introducing such concepts as 'variable geometry', 'flexibility' or 'multiple speed' of European integration. The Maastricht Treaty on European Union, for instance, provided a basis for the United Kingdom to opt-out of the Social Policy Chapter (→ *10.14, 10.16*), for the United Kingdom and Denmark to opt-out of the European Monetary Union (EMU), as well as allowing neutrals to opt-out of defence agreements, while the Nice Treaty contains reformed provisions on 'enhanced cooperation' between smaller circles of EU Member States. This, of course, may clearly jeopardise the ideal of a coherent 'acquis communautaire', that is, the entire body of Community law,

comprising the Community treaties, legislation, the case law of
the ECJ, as well as unwritten law such as general principles of
Community law.

When flexibility was introduced, it was well recognised that
an enlarged Union required different decision-making procedures in order to work effectively. Thus, in order to amend the
treaties, 'institutional reform' has been on the agenda of the
intergovernmental conferences (→ *1.8*) since Maastricht.

? 1.7 Which steps have been undertaken to widen the Community since the 1990s?

After the first enlargements of the three Communities in 1973
(Denmark, the United Kingdom and Ireland), 1981 (Greece),
and 1986 (Portugal and Spain), the accession of Austria,
Finland and Sweden in 1995 brought the European Union to a
membership of fifteen countries.

The true widening debate, however, related to the wave of
membership applications of the 1990s by Turkey and Morocco
(already in 1987), Cyprus and Malta (1990), Switzerland (1992),
Hungary and Poland (1994), Bulgaria, Romania, Slovakia,
Estonia, Lithuania and Latvia (1995), the Czech Republic and
Slovenia (1996).

The rules governing the **accession** of new Members to the
EU provide that any 'European State' that respects the principles of freedom, democracy, human rights and the rule of
law may apply for membership. After a preliminary assessment by the Commission (**'avis'**), the Council decides on the
opening of formal negotiations. There is not much substantive
leeway involved here because the EU regularly insists on the
acceptance by the accession candidates of the entire *'acquis
communautaire'* (→ *1.6*). Basically the negotiations may result
in the provision of transitional periods, effectively postponing

the entry-into-force of certain parts of the *acquis*. Next, the European Parliament, by an absolute majority of the MEPs, and the Council, by a unanimous vote, have to agree before all EU Member States have to ratify the accession treaty.

In practice, the EC/EU has used various forms of **pre-accession** treaties to prepare candidates for membership. The **Agreement on the European Economic Area** (EEA) with six EFTA states, which entered into force after protracted negotiations in 1994, is a – very sophisticated – example of an **association agreement** (→ *11.1, 11.3*) concluded by the EC. Only a year later, three states, namely Austria, Finland and Sweden, joined the EU, while Iceland, Liechtenstein and Norway remain 'associated' with the EC/EU through the EEA.

Between 1991 and 1996, another wave of association agreements, the so-called **Europe Agreements**, with the Eastern European countries in transition and **partnership agreements** with the Baltic States, Albania, the Russian Federation, Ukraine and other CIS states were concluded.

The Europe Agreements led to the biggest enlargement of the EU ever when ten new countries, namely Cyprus, the Czech Republic, Estonia, Hungary, Latvia, Lithuania, Malta, Poland, the Slovak Republic and Slovenia joined the Union in 2004. In 2007, Romania and Bulgaria acceded to the Union bringing its total membership to twenty-seven states.

The accession of Turkey, with which the EC has been linked through an association agreement since 1963, remains the most controversial politically.

? 1.8 Which were the major steps towards political union?

The grand political designs of the 'federalists' fared less well than the functional approach (→ *1.2*). In particular, the early plans for a European Defence and Political Community were unsuccessful.

In 1952, after the outbreak of the Korean War and under American pressure for German rearmament, the Treaty establishing a **European Defence Community** was signed. It was based on the French Pleven Plan and its intention was to integrate German military power in a way modelled on the ECSC structure. However, it never entered into force, because its ratification by France had become impossible after the French National Assembly rejected it in 1954. At the same time, early plans to set up a European Political Community ultimately failed. Also, later attempts to revive such ideas for a union of European States remained unsuccessful. While the Member States commissioned proposals for political union, the resulting Fouchet Plans (1961, 1962) were not adopted. Instead, again in a more pragmatic fashion, the EC Member States assumed a voluntary political cooperation on the basis of unanimity which has been called **European Political Cooperation** (EPC) since the 1970s (→ *11.14*). In this framework the heads of state or government of the Member States began to meet regularly in what was to be called the **European Council** (→ *2.2, 2.3*).

Other important steps on the way to **European political union** were the Tindemans Report of 1975 (which called for economic and monetary union, institutional reform, a common foreign policy, etc.), the first direct elections to the European Parliament and the creation of a European Monetary System in 1979, the Genscher–Colombo Plan of 1981 for the establishment of a European Union, and the Spinelli draft Treaty establishing the European Union adopted by the Parliament in 1984.

These events led to the two **intergovernmental conferences** (→ *1.6*) on economic and monetary union, on the one hand, and on political union, on the other, opened in 1990 and concluded by the 1992 Maastricht Treaty on European Union. This in turn provided the impetus for further intergovernmental conferences in 1996–1997 and in 2000, leading to the adoption of the Amsterdam Treaty and more recently the Nice Treaty, which entered into force on 1 February 2003.

? 1.9 What happened to the EU constitution?

All these developments served as input for the currently abandoned process of adopting a constitution for Europe. While a Constitutional Convention, a body composed of representatives of EU institutions as well as of national parliaments and governments both of Member States and accession candidates, produced a Draft Treaty establishing a Constitution for Europe, which was adopted by an Intergovernmental Conference of the Union's Member States and signed by them in 2004, French and Dutch voters openly rejected this further treaty amendment in national referenda. Since then the process of further 'constitutionalisation' or deepening of the Union has been held up.

The starting points for the deliberations in the Constitutional Convention were the 'left-overs' from the Nice Treaty, as laid down in the 2001 Laeken Declaration of the European Council: the division of powers between the EU and its Member States (→ 3.1, 3.3); the status of the EU Fundamental Rights Charter (→ 6.15); the simplification of the Treaties; and the role of national parliaments. The Draft Constitution Treaty suggested the merger of the separate pillars (→ 2.1) and the creation of one single EU with a more effective decision-making process and broader powers.

? 1.10 What is the Lisbon Reform Treaty?

In June 2007, the plans to adopt the Constitution Treaty were finally abandoned. Instead, a **Reform Treaty** was elaborated, which incorporated many features of the Draft Constitution but represented a clearly scaled-down version of the former. In December 2007, the Member States agreed on the **Lisbon Reform Treaty,** which would have amended both the EU and the EC Treaty, renaming the latter **'Treaty on the Functioning of the European Union'** and replacing the EC by the EU.

However, at the time of writing (September 2008), the Reform Treaty's future is also more than uncertain. The ratification process, well under way in most Member States, was slowed down and possibly came to halt when, in June 2008, Irish voters rejected the treaty in a popular referendum. As a consequence, the EU and EC are still governed by the treaties in the form resulting from the Nice Treaty amendments. The following chapters will try to answer some essential questions of EU law on this basis.

2 The institutional framework

The organisational structure of the EU/EC may, with all its complexity, seem Byzantine to outsiders. However, once the basic outline and the fundamental difference between the **intergovernmental EU** and the **supranational EC** are understood, it will become easier to find one's way. In particular, with regard to the EC, one will recognise an interesting mix between the traditional traits of an international organisation and those of a state-like entity with typical separation-of-powers issues.

According to Article 7 of the Treaty Establishing the European Community (TEC), the EC possesses five 'principal institutions': the **Council**; the **Commission**; the **European Parliament**; the **Court of Auditors**; and the **European Court of Justice**. In addition, a number of other advisory institutions, such as the **European Economic and Social Committee** or the **Committee of the Regions**, serve the 'organisation' EC. While the 'institutional triangle', consisting of the Council, Commission and Parliament and largely responsible for the Community's legislation, will be described in some detail in this chapter, the Community courts, the European Court of Justice, the Court of First Instance as well as the new Civil Service Tribunal, will be explained in chapter 5 (Judicial Control within the Community).

This section aims at explaining the **composition** and **internal decision making** of the Community institutions, while their interaction in the context of **European legislation** will be analysed in chapter 3 (The Making of Community Law).

? 2.1 Outline the structure of the EU

There is much confusion about the true subject(s) of European integration. Everything was originally quite simple and straight-forward. The Treaties of Rome (→ *1.3*) added the European Economic Community (EEC) and the European Atomic Energy Community (EURATOM) to the existing European Coal and Steel Community (ECSC) (→ *1.3*). In 1965, these three separate supranational organisations pooled their institutions in the so-called Merger Treaty (→ *1.5*), but otherwise they remained legally distinct entities. Over the years the short label 'European Community' (EC) gained acceptance not only for the EEC but also for all three Communities.

As so often happens, changes in the law followed the factual ones. In 1992, the Member States agreed to officially rename the European Economic Community (EEC) as the European Community (EC). The treaty by which they did so provided for a number of other very significant structural changes. After many failed attempts in the past, the Maastricht Treaty (Treaty on European Union (TEU)) (→ *1.6*, *1.8*, *2.3*, *11.1*, *11.14*) finally established a European Union (EU), which is based on three different pillars:

(1) the three supranational (→ *1.3*, *1.5*), pre-existing European Communities, as well as the two intergovernmental (→ *1.5*, *11.15*, *11.19*) pillars;
(2) Common Foreign and Security Policy (CFSP); and
(3) Co-operation in Justice and Home Affairs (JHA).

The latter initially covered such diverse fields as asylum, immigration, international crime issues, as well as judicial, customs and police cooperation. In 1997, some of these tasks were shifted to the supranational EC pillar by the Treaty of

Amsterdam, which also renamed the third pillar Police and Judicial Cooperation in Criminal Matters (PJCC).

A number of common provisions provide the roof structure of this 'European House'. It should not come as a surprise that the quasi-official classical image of a 'temple with three pillars' never gained universal acceptance and that some prefer to speak of the bizarre structure of a Gothic cathedral.

2.2 How and why is the Union 'served by a single institutional framework'?

Despite its complicated structure the TEU tries to streamline the institutional framework of the Union. The 'European Council' (→ *1.8*, *2.3*, *11.14*) composed of the heads of state or government of the Member States and the President of the Commission, is the only true EU organ, which according to Article 4 TEU 'shall provide the Union with the necessary impetus for its development and shall define the general political guidelines thereof'. Otherwise, the EC organs, in particular the Council and the Commission – 'on loan' from the EC – are also used to fulfil tasks of the EU. The rationale for this lies in an attempt to ensure the consistency of EU activities.

To complicate matters even further, the EC Council decided in 1993 to call itself 'Council of the EU'. It remains, however, an institution of the EC, sometimes operating in the framework of the EU.

These institutional intricacies, however, are not the only complications that may lead to disorientation among the non-initiated. The 1997 Amsterdam Treaty, driven by the mandate of Treaty simplification, brought some additional confusion by renumbering all the existing TEU and TEC Articles. Thus, one has to read pre-Amsterdam legislation and case law of the European courts with caution, being aware that the Treaty provisions referred to have been changed. One of the less attractive changes envisaged both by the **Draft Constitution Treaty** and the **Lisbon Reform Treaty** would have been another round of renumbering. Since both projects have failed the counting according to the Amsterdam Treaty remains valid.

2.3 What is the difference between the 'European Council' and the 'Council of the EU'?

The '**European Council**' ($\rightarrow$ 2.2, 11.14) is the only genuine EU institution. For the rest, the EU is served by the institutional framework of the EC. Evolving through a series of heads of government meetings since the 1960s, which were institutionalised at the Paris Summit in 1974, the 'European Council' was first mentioned in the Community treaties as a result of the 1986 **Single European Act** (SEA). It is now legally based on the TEU. According to its Article 4, it consists of the heads of state or government of the Member States and the President of the Commission, assisted by the Foreign Ministers and a Commission member. The European Council meets at least twice a year (in practice four times a year) and is entrusted with the broad policy definition of the Union. In the words of the TEU, it 'shall provide the Union with the necessary impetus for its development and shall define the general political guidelines thereof' ($\rightarrow$ 11.16).

As an EU institution the 'European Council' is not identical to the '**Council of the EU**'. That Council – originally the 'Council of the EC' or just the '**Council**' – is rather one of the five 'principal institutions' of the EC, receiving its somewhat misleading name from a 1993 Council Decision to rename itself ($\rightarrow$ 2.2). This was, of course, the result of the additional tasks it had received as a result of the Maastricht Treaty under the 'second' and 'third pillar' ($\rightarrow$ 2.1). According to Article 203 TEC, the

Council consists of a **representative** of each **Member State** 'at **ministerial level**, authorised to commit the government of that Member State'. This formulation was added by the Maastricht Treaty in order to allow also representatives of provinces of federal states to sit on the Council.

The **Presidency** (→*11.18, 11.20, 11.21*) of the Council, responsible for organising and chairing **Council**, **COREPER** (Permanent Representatives Committee) (→ *2.8*) and **working group** meetings, is held by each Member State for a period of six months.

2.4 Who represents the Member States in the Council?

The '**Council of the EU**', while always consisting of exactly the same Member States, is not always made up of the same representatives. Rather, the Member States are represented in this EC institution according to the **subject-matter** under consideration by 'a representative of each Member State at ministerial level'.

Thus, the **finance ministers** of the Member States meet as the '**Council for Economic and Financial Affairs**', commonly referred to as '**ECOFIN**', the environmental ministers as **Environmental Council**, while the foreign ministers constitute the so-called **General Affairs and External Relations Council**. As the External Relations Council the foreign ministers deal with **CFSP** issues (→ *11.17, 11.18*), while as the **General Affairs Council** they perform a mostly **coordinating** role and deal with cross-cutting Community policies, such as enlargement or budgetary questions, and prepare and follow up the European Council Meetings. In total, the Council meets in nine '**configurations**', comprising, in addition to the three mentioned above: 'Cooperation in the fields of Justice and Home Affairs'; 'Employment, Social Policy, Health and Consumer Affairs'; 'Competitiveness'; 'Transport,

Telecommunications and Energy'; Agriculture and Fisheries'; and 'Education, Youth and Culture'.

As a result of this multiplication, it may happen that a number of Council meetings take place simultaneously in different meeting rooms in Brussels or Luxembourg. Council meetings are always attended by Commission representatives at Commissioner level, who are assisted by a Secretariat headed by the Secretary-General of the Council (→ *11.21*).

? 2.5 Which voting procedures are followed in the Council?

As lawyers probably know, the correct answer to legal questions is, almost invariably: 'It depends'. This is also true for the procedure to be followed by the Council, which depends upon the precise legal basis on which it is empowered to act.

Broadly speaking, there are three main voting procedures available to the Council under Article 205 TEC:

(1) simple majority;
(2) qualified majority; and
(3) unanimity.

Simple majority voting requires the votes of fourteen out of the twenty-seven Member States. It applies in a subsidiary fashion, if the TEC does not provide otherwise, which leaves mainly procedural questions to this voting technique.

Qualified majority voting (QMV) (→ *3.5, 3.9*) has become the most important form of decision making within the Council. Today, most legislative acts, and especially those concerning the internal market (→ *7.7*), have become subject to QMV.

Unanimity presently applies only in very sensitive and important areas or where the Council seeks to depart from the position of the other law-making institutions, that is, the

Commission and Parliament. Unanimity remains the rule in the intergovernmental second and third pillar, that is, the CFSP and the PJCC (→ *2.1, 11.19*).

Article 205(3) TEC provides that Members, either present in person or represented, may abstain without preventing the adoption of acts requiring unanimity. This formulation, therefore, indicates that unanimous decisions may not be taken if one of the Members is absent. In the past, the predecessor rule to this provision has been used by some Members, most notably by France exercising its 'empty chair' policy in the 1960s by which it prevented the Community from adopting acts, in particular, in the controversial Common Agricultural Policy (CAP) (→ *2.7, 10.1–3*).

? 2.6 Outline the development and prospects of qualified majority voting

The number of votes each Member State can cast, as well as the number of votes constituting a qualified majority, is set by the Treaty. While the allocation of votes to individual Member States roughly corresponds to such 'objective' factors as economic power, population and geographical size, the precise figures remain subject to political bargaining.

After the 1995 accession of three more Member States (→ *1.7*), QMV was defined as sixty-two out of a total of eighty-seven votes, cast by all (then) fifteen EC Members. Under this system of weighted voting the largest Members (Germany, France, Italy and the UK) had ten votes, Spain eight, Belgium, Greece, the Netherlands and Portugal five, Austria and Sweden four, Denmark, Ireland and Finland three and Luxembourg two votes. Where, exceptionally, a vote was not taken on the basis of a Commission proposal an additional requirement was that ten Member States had to vote in favour.

As a result of the 2004 accession of ten new EU Member States the allocation of votes and the required voting quorums had to be amended again. The Enlargement Protocol inserted the necessary changes to Article 205 TEC, which distributed votes ranging between three (for Malta) and twenty-nine (for Germany, France and the UK). The new quorum for a qualified majority was 232 votes, cast by a majority of Members in the case of a vote on a Commission proposal. In other cases, a two-thirds majority of Member States is additionally required.

The 2004 enlargement has also introduced the idea of a so-called **triple majority** in certain cases. A new paragraph 4 was inserted into Article 205 TEC according to which, in the case of a qualified majority voting, 'a member of the Council may request verification that the Member States constituting the qualified majority represent at least 62% of the total population of the Union. If that condition is shown not to have been met, the decision in question shall not be adopted.'

The bargaining about the allocation of votes and the precise technique of QMV remains one of the most contentious negotiating issues, not only at each round of enlargement but also whenever Treaty amendments are discussed. Thus, the question was also prominent during the Convention debates on the European **Constitution Treaty**. According to the (provisional) compromise found by the **Intergovernmental Conference** ($\rightarrow$ *1.9*) in Article I-25(1) Draft Constitution Treaty, a 'qualified majority shall be defined as at least 55% of the members of the Council, comprising at least fifteen of them and representing Member States comprising at least 65% of the population of the Union'. With the rejection of the Draft Constitution Treaty it is highly uncertain whether this formula will ever be adopted in practice.

As of 1 January 2007, after the accession of Romania and Bulgaria (with fourteen and ten votes, respectively), the total

number of votes has risen to 345. Under the new voting requirements, a qualified majority is reached by 255 votes in favour,
which amounts to approximately 74% of the total number of
votes. In addition, a majority of Member States – in some cases
even a two-thirds majority of Member States – is required to
adopt a Council measure.

2.7 What did the 'Luxembourg Compromise' achieve?

By the 'Luxembourg Compromise' or 'Luxembourg Accord',
the Member States managed to solve a severe political crisis in
1966, when France exercised its so-called empty chair policy (→
2.5) preventing Council decisions from being made on **Common
Agricultural Policy** (CAP) issues.

The political compromise achieved basically enabled a single
Member State to request a departure from majority voting (→
2.5, 2.6) by invoking its essential interests. In diplomatic language it provided:

> Where, in the case of decisions which may be taken by
> majority vote on a proposal of the Commission, very
> important interests of one or more partners are at stake,
> the Members of the Council will endeavour, within a
> reasonable time, to reach solutions which can be adopted
> by all the members of the Council while respecting
> their mutual interests and those of the Community, in
> accordance with Article 2 of the EEC Treaty.

France added that discussions should continue until unanimity can be reached, while other Member States thought that
prolonged inability to arrive at a mutually acceptable solution
would lead back to majority voting.

The legal implications of this undertaking, which has not

at any time become part of treaty or secondary EC law, were never formally tested. While it probably constituted just a non-binding, political agreement (a gentlemen's agreement), some have argued that it might have had an *estoppel* effect, preventing Member States from suddenly changing their voting behaviour. The Luxembourg Accord was invoked a few times in the context of the CAP during the 1980s; however, it is no longer directly relevant today. It did find some re-incarnation in the so-called Joannina formula which provided for an informal strengthening of the blocking minority after the 1995 accession round.

The 'Luxembourg Compromise' continues to serve as an important reminder of the inherent tension between supranational (QMV) and intergovernmental (unanimity) decision-making procedures (→ *1.3*, *1.5*). Thus, it is not surprising that it found a recent re-incarnation in the context of the CFSP's first timid attempts to introduce QMV in its decision-making procedures in Article 23(2) TEU (→ *11.19*).

? 2.8 Explain the structure and tasks of COREPER

The Permanent Representatives Committee, better known under its French acronym 'COREPER', consists of the diplomatic representatives of the Member States to the EU in Brussels. It is their task to prepare the work of the Council.

As a subsidiary body of the Council, COREPER meets at two levels: COREPER II, usually consisting of the permanent representatives of the Member States at ambassador level, deals with the most important matters such as economic and finance issues or external relations; and COREPER I, normally staffed by the deputies of the permanent representatives, addresses issues such as the environment, social affairs or the internal market.

If the representatives within COREPER reach consensus, that is, an informal agreement, then there will be no deliberation of these items, so-called A-points, in the Council. Rather, they will be adopted through a simplified bloc vote. The remaining issues, so-called B-points, will be discussed and decided upon in the Council by the ministers according to the voting procedures provided for in the Treaty (→ 2.5).

COREPER in turn is assisted by a number of working groups, composed of government officials from the Member States, as well as by many committees established under the 'comitology' scheme of the Treaties (→ 2.15).

The technical and organisational details of COREPER II meetings are prepared by the so-called *Antici* Group, the personal assistants of the permanent representatives and, in the case of COREPER I, by the so-called *Mertens* Group.

All these groupings on a sub-ministerial level are crucial for the functioning of the Council; they serve to integrate Member States' interests in the EU's decision-making process and they help to transmit European interests back to the Member State level.

? 2.9 How many nationals of the same Member State can serve on the Commission?

Though the members of the Commission serve in their personal capacity and are not supposed to represent Member State interests, the question of whether all Member States would continue to have the right to nominate their 'national Commissioner' has been one of the most controversial issues during the enlargement negotiations of the 1990s and in the early years after the turn of the millennium.

Until the 2004 accession of ten new Members, the five largest Member States, namely France, Germany, Italy, Spain and the

UK, had in fact kept their right to nominate two members of the Commission. Since that time the Commission has included only one national of each of the Member States.

The 2004 Enlargement Protocol provides, however, that after the accession of the twenty-seventh Member State the number of members of the Commission shall be less than the number of Member States. It continues stating that the '[m]embers of the Commission shall be chosen according to a rotation system based on the principle of equality, the implementing arrangements for which shall be adopted by the Council, acting unanimously'. In other words, since an acceptable decision on a rotation system could not be agreed upon in 2004 this decision was deferred to a later stage.

The current twenty-seven Commissioners are chosen on the 'grounds of their **general competence** and whose **independence** is beyond doubt', as Article 213(1) TEC puts it. According to Article 214(1) TEC, they serve **renewable five-year terms**.

The members of the Commission are assisted by a personal staff, called a **'cabinet'**, of usually six (for the President, nine) people and by permanent officials working in the **Directorates-General** (DGs) organised according to subject-matter areas similar to ministries at the national level.

2.10 How are the members of the Commission selected?

Over the years, the procedure of setting up the Commission has been significantly refined. In particular, the role of the Parliament in the process of choosing Commissioners has been strengthened. According to Article 214(2) TEC, the Council, meeting in the composition of heads of state or government and acting by a qualified majority, **nominates** the person it wishes to appoint as **President** of the Commission. With the approval of the Parliament to this nomination, it will then, by **common accord with the nominee** for President and on the basis of the **proposals** made **by each Member State**, nominate the other members of the Commission. As a next step, these nominees and the prospective President 'as a body' are subject to a **'vote of approval'** by the **Parliament** after which they are **'appointed by the Council, acting by a qualified majority'.**

In practice, the Parliament has conducted hearings with nominees and, if dissatisfied with individual candidates, threatened to veto the entire Commission. In 2004 this led to the replacement of three nominees of the Barroso Commission.

? 2.11 How is a Commission proposal adopted?

According to Article 219 TEC, the Commission takes decisions by **simple majority** voting. In practice, formal votes are taken in the weekly Commission meetings only very rarely. Rather, a number of other procedures are used in order to adopt numerous Commission decisions. Pursuant to the **written procedure**, proposals are communicated to the Commission members, who may raise reservations and/or amendments. Otherwise, the proposal will be adopted as suggested. According to the **empowerment procedure**, the college of Commissioners may empower one or more of its members to make a decision, while the **delegation procedure** allows a transfer of decision-making powers to directors-general and heads of service.

Since the Commission is a **collegiate body**, once decisions are taken they have to be backed by the entire Commission. This is sometimes referred to as the principle of collegiality or of collective responsibility.

2.12 Describe the elements of the Commission's 'right of initiative'

The Commission has the **exclusive right** to formulate legislative **proposals** of the Community (→ *3.4*). There are only very few exceptions such as budgetary matters or issues concerning a uniform election law for the European Parliament. However, the 'monopoly' of initiative of the Commission exists only in the first (Community) pillar, and not with regard to the CFSP or Justice and Home Affairs (→ *2.1*). Legally, the right of initiative results from the fact that most Treaty provisions calling for Community legislation expressly require the Council to act **'on a proposal from the Commission'**. This gives the Commission enormous influence not only on the actual formulation, but ultimately also on the content of Community legislation.

In practice, the importance of the Commission's right of initiative is reinforced by the fact that Council amendments of such proposals usually require unanimity, and by the right of the Commission to amend or withdraw proposals at any time before actual Council adoption.

Further, only the Council and Parliament can request the Commission to submit proposals. The Commission, however, has no corresponding duty to act upon any such requests.

2.13 How does the Commission fulfil its tasks of supervision and control?

The Commission acts as the **'guardian of the treaties'** ensuring that EU/EC law is complied with. For this purpose, the TEC endows the Commission with a number of specific supervisory powers, ultimately comprising the power to institute legal proceedings before the ECJ in a variety of cases such as:

- the **right to sue a Member State** according to Article 226 TEC (→ *5.11*);
- the **right to sue other Community organs** according to Article 230 TEC (→ *5.6*); and
- the **right to request a lump sum or penalty payment** from Member States failing to implement a decision of the ECJ according to Article 228(2) TEC (→ *5.12*).

Furthermore, for a long time the Commission was directly responsible for 'enforcing' competition law under Articles 81 and 82 TEC (→ *9.16*). Even after the reform of EC competition law, it has retained certain supervisory powers under Regulation 1/2003/EC.

? 2.14 What is the Commission's role in the Community's external relations?

In the field of the Community's 'foreign affairs', called 'external relations' in EC jargon, the Commission shares powers with the Council which, most importantly, retains the power to conclude **international agreements** entered into by the EC (→ *11.1*).

Such agreements are, however, **negotiated** by the Commission, albeit under certain Council influence laid down in Article 300 TEC: basically, the Council must authorise the Commission to open negotiations. In addition, the Council may appoint a special committee to assist the Commission and it may issue directives to the Commission for the conduct of negotiations. The Commission's negotiating role is particularly important in the high-profile case of the accession of new Member States (→ *11.3*).

Further, the **Commission represents** the EC in the World Trade Organization (WTO) and in other **international organisations**, such as the United Nations and its specialized agencies, the Council of Europe, OECD and others (→ *11.1*); it also maintains diplomatic ties with more than 140 countries accredited to the EU.

Based on the **Common Commercial Policy** powers under Article 133 TEC, the Commission is also in charge of enforcing the EC's trade protection legislation, such as anti-dumping and countervailing duty legislation or the Trade Barriers Regulation (→ *11.2*).

2.15 Does the comitology system distort the Community's institutional balance?

The notion of '**comitology**' basically signifies a complicated system of law-making under the supervision of specialised committees, which represent Member States and assist the Commission in areas of law-making delegated by the Council (→ *2.8*). To a considerable extent, comitology applies in the fields of agriculture (→ *10.1*), fisheries (→ *10.6*) and competition law → *ch. 9*).

According to the Comitology Decision 1999/468/EC, one has to distinguish between so-called:

- **advisory committees,** which have only consultative functions;
- **management committees,** whose qualified majority rejection of a Commission draft refers the matter to the Council; and
- **regulatory committees,** whose approval is required for the Commission.

Because of the vast transfer of law-making powers from the Council to the Commission (more than two-thirds of all regulations are adopted under delegated law-making procedures), comitology has been questioned repeatedly from a constitutional point of view as possibly threatening the institutional balance between Council and Commission and the rights of the European Parliament.

Though there was no authority for 'comitology' in the original Treaty text, the ECJ upheld the legality of this system in 1970 in Case 25/70 *Einfuhr- und Vorratsstelle* v. *Köster et al.* [1970] ECR 1161. Basically, the Court found that if the Treaty gave the Council the power to delegate law-making powers it could do so with conditions. This reasoning was integrated into the text of the Treaty by the **SEA** ($\rightarrow$*2.3*) which amended Article 145 (now Article 202) TEC. In addition to its authority to confer on the Commission certain rule-making powers, it expressly stated that the Council 'may impose certain requirements in respect of the exercise of these powers'.

? 2.16 Describe the structure of the European Parliament

The **'Assembly'**, as it was originally referred to in the ECSC and EC Treaty, began to refer to itself as **'Parliament'** in 1962. Since the 1986 SEA it has officially been known as the **'European Parliament'** (EP).

Currently, the EP consists of 785 members (MEPs), ranging from ninety-nine from Germany to five from Malta, who, since 1979, have been directly elected for a **five-year term** on the basis of the respective national election laws. Though there are no genuine European political parties as yet, MEPs are organised not according to national but rather according to **transnational party affiliations** in: the EPP–ED (Group of the European People's Party (Christian Democrats) and European Democrats); the PES (Group of the Party of European Socialists); the ALDE (Alliance of Liberals and Democrats for Europe); Les Verts/The Greens/EFA (Group of the Greens/European Free Alliance);

the GUE/NGL (Confederal Group of the European United Left/Nordic Green Left); the UEN (Union for Europe of the Nations Group); or the IND/DEM (Independence/Democracy Group in the European Parliament).

After some disagreement and rivalry over the official seat of the Parliament, in 1992 the Member States decided that plenary sessions would take place in Strasbourg, committee meetings in Brussels and that the Secretariat should be seated in Luxembourg.

Parliamentary sessions are chaired by an elected president and by fourteen vice-presidents (each for a term of 2½ years), who form the EP's 'Bureau', the Parliament's executive body in charge of internal financial, administrative and organisational matters. In addition, the president chairs the Conference of Presidents, composed of the leaders of the political groups, a body which decides, among other things, on the agenda for plenary meetings, bringing suit against another institution before the ECJ (→ 5.6) and settling conflicts of jurisdiction between different parliamentary committees.

Most of the work of the EP is carried out in its twenty special-ised standing committees (for example, legal affairs and citizens' rights, foreign affairs, petitions, etc.), wherein MEPs serving as rapporteurs will draft parliamentary resolutions expressing the EP's opinion on Commission proposals. These parliamentary committees of twenty-eight to eighty-six members meet once or twice a month in public sessions in Brussels in order to discuss legislative proposals.

2.17 What are the legislative 'powers' of the European Parliament?

The EP is not a true legislator. Rather, as it is nicely put in Article 192 of the EC Treaty, it 'shall participate in the process leading up to the adoption of Community acts' (→ *ch. 3*). Today, the two most important law-making procedures are consultation (→ *3.5*) and co-decision (→ *3.7*). The cooperation (→ *3.6*) and the assent (→ *2.19, 3.8*) procedure, together with many other more specialised procedures are used less frequently. Which particular procedure applies and what areas may be regulated is determined by the Treaty provision containing the legal basis for the specific piece of legislation.

The fact that today most economic issues concerning the internal market are subject to the co-decision procedure, which implies a *de facto* veto power for the EP, means that the Parliament has become an important player in the process of European legislation.

? 2.18 How does the Parliament exercise control vis-à-vis the other European institutions?

The Parliament's relatively weak law-making powers are partly compensated for by a full range of supervisory powers, similar to those that can be found in national parliaments. In particular, the EP has the right to:

*   approve of nominations of Commission president and members (Article 214 TEC) (→ *2.10*);
*   cast a vote of no-confidence, a so-called motion of censure, by a two-thirds majority on the Commission 'as a body' (Article 201 TEC);
*   question the Commission (Article 197 TEC) and to some extent the Council;
*   bring an action for annulment or failure to act (Articles 230 and 232 TEC) (→ *5.6, 5.4*); and
*   set up a temporary Committee of Inquiry (Article 195 TEC).

In addition, the EP has appointed an **Ombudsman** (Article 195 TEC) to receive complaints concerning 'instances of maladministration' within the EU institutions, and the Treaty provides for the right of any individual to petition the EP (Article 194 TEC) on matters within the Community's fields of activity and which directly affect him or her.

2.19 Which situations require the assent of the European Parliament?

The **assent**, sometimes also called **approval**, procedure ($\rightarrow$ *2.17*) is required for a number of highly important matters such as:

- the **accession** of new Member States under Article 49(1) TEU ($\rightarrow$ *1.7, 11.3*);
- the conclusion of so-called **association agreements** according to Article 310 TEC pursuant to Article 300(3) TEC ($\rightarrow$ *11.1, 11.11*); and
- the **investiture** of the Commission according to Article 214 TEC ($\rightarrow$ *2.10*).

2.20 What is the Parliament's role in the Community's budgetary process?

According to Article 272 TEC, the **EP**, together with the **Council**, **approves** of the annual **budget** based on a **Commission proposal** in a budgetary procedure during which it may make changes and amendments to the initial proposal. The annual budget is funded from so-called **'own resources'** of the Community, which comprise: **customs duties** based on the Common Customs Tariff ($\rightarrow$ *11.2*); **agricultural levies**, charged on agricultural imports according to the CAP ($\rightarrow$ *10.3*); the so-called **'VAT resource'**, a contribution by the Member States equivalent to

1 per cent of the final selling price of a common base of goods and services, and the so-called 'GNP resource', a maximum of 1.27 per cent of a Member's GNP.

2.21 What does the Court of Auditors do?

The Court of Auditors consists of one national from each Member State appointed after consultation with the EP by the Council for a renewable six-year term. Pursuant to Article 248 TEC, it **examines** the accounts of all **revenue and expenditure** of the Community on the basis of the principles of **legality, regularity and sound financial management**. At the end of each fiscal year the Court of Auditors prepares the Annual Report on the basis of which the EP will give a discharge to the Commission.

2.22 What are the tasks of the European Economic and Social Committee as well as of the Committee of the Regions?

The Economic and Social Committee (ESC), which has started to call itself **European Economic and Social Committee (EESC)**, is not an 'institution' according to Article 7 TEC, but only an advisory 'side-institution' of the EC. Pursuant to Article 257 TEC, it enjoys 'advisory status' and consists of a maximum of 350 'representatives of the various economic and social components of organised civil society, and in particular representatives of producers, farmers, carriers, workers, dealers, craftsmen, professional occupations, consumers and the general interest'. The idea is to have an input from these various fields of organised civil society into the law-making process of the EC. The EC Treaty contains sometimes obligatory or optional **consultation** rights of the ESC, which also has the right of issuing opinions on its own initiative.

Like the ESC the **Committee of the Regions** may be consulted by the Commission, the Council or the EP during the law-making process of the EC, particularly on matters of **cross-border cooperation**. In practice, its influence appears to be rather low.

3 The making of Community law

Community law, that is, the law of the **supranational** organisation **European Community**, consists of so-called primary and secondary law. The concept of **primary law** relates to law made by the Member States via their international law treaty-making powers. Therefore, it comprises the initial 1957 Treaty of Rome plus various treaty amendments, such as the SEA, the Maastricht, Amsterdam and Nice Treaties, as well as the accession treaties. **Secondary law**, on the other hand, refers to law **made by** the Community's **institutions** based on the authorisation contained in the Treaties (the primary law), such as regulations, directives and decisions, as well as soft-law instruments such as recommendations and opinions.

Article 249 TEC briefly characterises the legal quality of these **legislative instruments**:

> In order to carry out their task and in accordance with the provisions of this Treaty, the European Parliament acting jointly with the Council, the Council and the Commission shall make regulations and issue directives, take decisions, make recommendations or deliver opinions.
>
> A **regulation** shall have **general application**. It shall be **binding** in its entirety and **directly applicable** in all Member States.
>
> A **directive** shall be **binding**, as to the **result to be achieved**, upon each Member State to which it is

> addressed, but shall leave to the national authorities the choice of form and methods.
>
> A decision shall be binding in its entirety upon those to whom it is addressed.
>
> Recommendations and opinions shall have no binding force.

In the field of Justice and Home Affairs, the third EU pillar, framework decisions, fulfil the function of directives, while decisions are used for purposes other than harmonisation.

The Draft Constitution Treaty intended to replace the somewhat technocratic terminology of legislative acts by some more generally comprehensible terms. Instead of regulations 'European laws', instead of directives 'European framework laws' and instead of decisions 'European decisions' would have been adopted. Further, draft Article I-33(1) CT would have introduced a 'European regulation' more akin to administrative regulations used by many national executive branches rather than the current EC regulations.

In addition to the non-binding recommendations and opinions, a number of soft law instruments have been used. They range from Action Plans, outlining intended legislation, and Declarations, laying down certain procedures or values to be respected, to soft law-making procedures, such as the 'open method of coordination' used in various fields not covered by Community competence. Through this method of policy coordination 'best practices' are identified, which other Member States are encouraged to emulate, and their performance is then often 'benchmarked' against that of the most successful. The open method of coordination has frequently been applied, particularly in the field of social and employment policy.

3.1 What does the principle of 'conferral' or 'enumerated powers' stand for?

The Treaties do not contain a general grant of legislative powers to the EC/EU. Instead, the principle of 'enumerated' or 'conferred powers' means that all powers enjoyed by the Community or the Union are 'derived powers', which have been transferred from the Member States in the Treaties (→ *5.4, 5.8*). This idea is codified in Article 5(1) TEC which states:

> The Community shall act within the limits of the powers conferred upon it by this Treaty and of the objectives assigned to it therein.

The same concept of a limited transfer of powers is expressed in Article 7(1) TEC which provides that 'each institution shall act within the limits of the powers conferred upon it by this Treaty' (→ *5.8*).

This fairly obvious principle requiring delegated law-making by the EC institutions to be based on a Treaty authorisation is, however, complicated by the fact that the Treaty does not only contain express authorisations. Instead – and the ECJ has confirmed this position – Community legislation may also be based on 'implied powers' or on the broad authorisation contained in Article 308 TEC.

According to the **implied powers doctrine**, as developed primarily in the institutional law of the United Nations, international organisations are deemed to have such **powers** as are **necessary** for the **fulfilment** of their **functions**. Sometimes an even broader version of implied powers is used when, instead of 'functions', general 'treaty objectives' are taken as a yardstick to determine the scope of implied powers. The implied powers doctrine is also often relied upon in the area of **EC treaty-making powers** (→ *11.5–10*).

Despite a rather broad interpretation of Community powers – intended to give the Treaty the most effective application (*effet utile*) – the ECJ, in principle, seems to adhere to the narrower interpretation of implied powers. This can be seen in the case concerning *Migration Policies,* Joined Cases 281, 283–285 and 287–285 *Germany and others* v. *Commission* [1987] ECR 3203, in which the ECJ held that 'where an Article of the EEC Treaty . . . confers a specific task on the Commission it must be accepted, if that provision is not to be rendered wholly ineffective, that it confers on the Commission necessarily and *per se* the powers which are indispensable in order to carry out that task'.

The Court has demonstrated that it is willing to call a halt on too sweeping interpretations of Community powers by the institutions themselves. In the case concerning the Tobacco Advertising Directive, Case C-376/98 *Germany* v. *European Parliament and Council* [2000] ECR I-8419, it held that the Community legislature had no power to adopt that directive on the basis of the harmonisation provisions relating to the establishment of the internal market contained in Article 100a (now Article 95) TEC ($\rightarrow$ *5.8*). Thus, in a very rare move, the Tobacco Advertising Directive was annulled.

In addition to implied powers as accepted by the ECJ, the Treaty contains a very broad law-making authorisation in **Article 308 TEC** which runs as follows:

> If **action** by the Community should prove **necessary** to **attain**, in the course of the operation of the **common market**, one of the **objectives** of the Community, and this treaty has not provided the necessary powers, the Council shall, acting unanimously on a proposal from the Commission and after consulting the European Parliament, take the appropriate measures.

In the past, this provision has been used repeatedly by the EC in order to legislate in fields not yet covered by express authorisation, such as environmental policy measures ($\rightarrow$ *10.8*).

The fears concerning Article 308 TEC have been captured in the 2001 Laeken Declaration on Future Reform of the EU ($\rightarrow$ *1.9*). It opened up the possibility of a review of Article 308 in the light of preventing 'creeping expansion of competences' of the EU, and it enabled the Union to 'continue to be able to react to fresh challenges and developments and to explore new policy areas'.

As a reaction to these concerns, the Draft Constitution Treaty codified a catalogue of Community competences and reaffirmed the 'principle of conferral' in Article I-11 CT, as well as the, mainly judge-made, differentiation between exclusive Community/Union competences, shared competences and Member State competences ($\rightarrow$ *3.3*, *11.8*, *11.9*). At present, however, the ECJ's case law governs.

? 3.2 May the Council base a specific legal act on the Treaty as a whole?

The policy rationale of the principle of enumerated or conferred powers could be easily circumvented in practice if EC institutions invoked the Treaty in general as a legal basis of their law-making activities. Article 253 TEC aims at preventing such abuse by imposing a duty to state the reasons on which specific legislation is based ($\rightarrow$ *5.9*). The ECJ interpreted this obligation to require either specific reference to a Treaty article, or at least a possibility of identification from the context. In the case concerning *Tariff Preferences*, Case 45/86 *Commission v. Council* [1987] ECR 1493, the Court annulled ($\rightarrow$ *5.5*, *5.8*) a Council measure the legal basis of which had not been sufficiently identified.

The Treaty requirement to give reasons is intended to facilitate judicial review by the European courts and to foster transparency of law-making, which includes the opportunity for the parties to defend their rights and interests, as the ECJ has already found in Case 24/62 *Germany* v. *Commission* [1963] ECR 63 (→ *5.9*).

3.3 Explain the meaning of subsidiarity

To some extent as a response to the ever increasing scope of Community legislation, the principle of **subsidiarity** was introduced into the Treaties by the Maastricht amendments in 1992 in order to alleviate Member States' fears of the perceived creeping **expansion** of EC/EU **competences**.

As already enunciated in Article 2 TEU, the Community exercises its powers in accordance with the principle of subsidiarity, which has found a rather cryptic formulation in Article 5(2) TEC:

> In areas which do **not** fall within its **exclusive competence**, the Community shall take action, in accordance with the principle of subsidiarity, only if and insofar as the objectives of the proposed action **cannot** be **sufficiently achieved** by the Member States and can therefore, by reason of the scale or effects of the proposed action, be **better achieved** by the **Community**.

According to the 1997 Amsterdam Protocol on the Application of the Principles of Subsidiarity and Proportionality, the Commission is required to publish annual reports (under the title of '**Better Lawmaking'**) on the application of the principle.

Although in principle the ECJ has affirmed its power to annul Community acts adopted in violation of the principle of subsidiarity, and thereby accepted the latter's so-called **justiciability**, it has been very **reluctant** to second-guess the political agreement underlying Community legislation. This may have been one of the reasons why the Draft Constitution would have set up an early warning mechanism according to which national parliaments could request the Community institutions to reconsider proposed legislation they believe to be in violation of subsidiarity.

3.4 Outline the general principles of Community law-making

As a rule, Community legislation begins with a **Commission proposal** (this is usually referred to as the Commission's 'right of initiative' (→ *2.12*)), followed by Council deliberations with different degrees of **involvement** on the part of the **European Parliament** (→ *2.17*) and other **advisory bodies**, such as the Economic and Social Committee or the Committee of the Regions (→ *2.22*). What is ultimately required is the formal **adoption** of the proposal **by the Council** through qualified majority or unanimity (→ *2.5, 2.6*).

The Treaty contains a complex web of different **law-making procedures,** and it is sometimes very difficult to ascertain which would be the correct one to apply for a specific legislative proposal. In theory at least, the Treaty itself determines which of the different procedures applies to a particular subject-matter. Though there are a considerable number of different procedures in total, there are six main procedures of which the **consultation** (→ *3.5*) and the **co-decision** (→ *3.7*) procedures, as well as Council **legislation without parliamentary consultation** (→*3.8*) are the most important.

3.5 Does the consultation procedure still play a role in EU law-making?

The consultation procedure, as the major law-making procedure under the original 1957 Rome Treaty, gave only a modest role to the EP in Community law-making. It basically required the Council, before adopting a Commission proposal, either by QMV or unanimity, to obtain an opinion from the Parliament, although it did not have to follow it.

The ECJ has tried to interpret the procedural requirements in a strict manner to the advantage of the Parliament. In the *Isoglucose* case, Case 138/79 *Roquette Frères* v. *Council* [1980] ECR 3333, it held, for instance, that the Council's obligation to wait for the EP's opinion constituted an 'essential procedural safeguard', disregard of which led to the annulment of Council legislation (→ 5.9). In another case, the so-called *Generalised Tariff Preferences* case, Case C-65/93 *Parliament* v. *Council* [1995] ECR I-643, it held that, although there were no fixed deadlines, sufficient time is required for the EP so that only in urgent cases would the Council be allowed not to await the Parliament's opinion. In the *Road Taxes* case, Case C-21/94 *Parliament* v. *Council* [1996] ECR I-1827, the ECJ further clarified that there was a duty to re-consult the EP 'when the text finally adopted, viewed as a whole, departs substantially from the text on which the Parliament has already been consulted, except where the amendments essentially correspond to [its] wishes'.

Today, the most important use of the consultation procedure lies in the Community's harmonisation powers, officially called the 'approximation of laws for the functioning of the common market', provided for in Article 94 TEC (→ 8.20) and in the Community's gap-filling competence with regard to the common market in accordance with Article 308 TEC (→ 3.1). In addition, the consultation procedure applies, among others, in the following areas: certain non-discrimination legislation (Article 13 TEC) (→ *10.14*); rights to vote and stand in municipal and EP elections (Article 19 TEC); enhancement of citizenship rights (Article 22 TEC); state aid (Article 89 TEC) (→ *9.33*); harmonisation of indirect taxation (Article 93) (→ *7.12*); and the conclusion of international agreements (Article 300(3) TEC) (→ *11.3*).

3.6 Describe the co-operation procedure and its relevance to today's Community law making

The co-operation procedure according to Article 252 TEC was introduced by the SEA in 1986 (→ *2.3*). This could be seen as an acknowledgement of the EP's increased democratic legitimacy after the first direct elections in 1979 giving the Parliament a greater say in Community legislation (→ *2.16*). In a complex procedural system the cooperation procedure provides for two readings: a 'common position' to be adopted by the Council on the basis of the Parliament's opinion on the Commission proposal; and the requirement of unanimity in the Council if Parliament should be overruled.

Basically, the co-operation procedure builds on the earlier consultation procedure. After a first consultation of the EP (first reading), the Council informs the EP of the reasons to adopt a common position. Parliament then has three months after which it may either:

(1) approve of the common position by simple majority (it can do so implicitly by taking no position);
(2) propose amendments to the common position by absolute majority of its members; or
(3) reject the common position equally by absolute majority.

In the first case, the Council may then adopt the measure as contained in the common position. In case the Parliament proposes amendments, the Commission will re-examine the original proposal in the light of the Parliament's amendments, which it may accept or not. The Council may then adopt the re-examined proposal which incorporates the Parliament's amendments by qualified majority. Unanimity is, however, required in the Council if it wishes to adopt the EP's amendments which were not accepted in the Commission's re-examination or if it wants to again change the re-examined proposal.

Also in the final case of a parliamentary rejection of the common position the Council may adopt the act only by unanimity within three months. In practice, the Parliament rarely rejects common positions by the Council. Rather, it is good at getting its amendments accepted by the Council.

The **co-operation procedure** initially applied to a considerable number of legislative measures to be adopted in the field of the single market, among them Article 100a (now Article 95) TEC (measures to achieve the internal market) and Article 57 (now Article 47) TEC (directives on the mutual recognition of diplomas), as well as to environmental measures (ex Article 130s(1) TEC), health and safety for workers (ex Article 118a TEC) and social policy measures under the Social Policy Protocol (→ *10.16*). With the Maastricht and the Amsterdam Treaty these areas now have all become subject to the co-decision procedure, leaving only certain issues concerning the **European Monetary Union** for co-operation.

? 3.7 How does co-decision work?

With the amendments of the Treaty of Amsterdam a large portion of important Community law making is now subject to the so-called **co-decision procedure** according to Article 251 TEC. The importance of this procedure is underlined by the fact that the Draft Constitution Treaty and the Lisbon Reform Treaty simply refer to it as the **'legislative procedure'**. It reflects a further development of the cooperation procedure, and was first introduced by the Maastricht Treaty and modified by the Treaty of Amsterdam. It basically provides for **two successive readings**, by Parliament and the Council, of a Commission proposal and the convocation, if the two co-legislators cannot agree, of a **'Conciliation Committee'**. This is composed of Council and Parliament representatives, with the participation of the Commission, and should help to reach an agreement. Parliament may ultimately block the adoption through its veto.

Under this procedure a **Commission proposal** is sent to both the Parliament and the Council. If the Parliament does not propose any amendments, and if the Council accepts them all, it may adopt the proposal accordingly. Otherwise the Council shall adopt a **common position**. Parliament then has three months after which it may either:

(1) approve of the common position;
(2) reject the common position by absolute majority of its members; or
(3) propose amendments to the common position equally by absolute majority.

In the first case, the act will be deemed to have been adopted in accordance with the common position. In the second case, if Parliament exercises its **'veto power'**, the proposed act will be deemed not to have been adopted. In the case of parliamentary amendments, on which the Commission shall deliver its opinion, the following steps may occur:

(1) If the Council approves of all amendments by qualified majority, the act will be deemed to have been adopted accordingly (subject, however, to the qualification that the adoption of

amendments on which the Commission has delivered a negative opinion is only possible by a unanimous vote).

(2) If, however, the Council does not approve of all the amendments of the EP, the President of the Council, in agreement with the President of the EP, shall convene within six weeks a meeting of the **Conciliation Committee**. This committee, consisting of an equal number of representatives of the Council and the EP, has the task of reconciling the disagreement and agreeing on a joint text. Failure to reach such a joint text will lead to the lapse of the legislative proposal.

(3) If the Conciliation Committee does, however, approve a joint text within six weeks, Parliament and Council have another six weeks in which they may, by absolute majority of votes cast and by qualified majority, respectively, adopt the act in accordance with the joint text.

The **co-decision procedure** was initially intended for measures in the fields of harmonisation (former Articles 100a, 100b TEC), free movement of workers, the freedom of establishment, education, culture, public health and consumer protection and is now, particularly after the changes introduced by the Treaty of Amsterdam, applicable to a wide variety of areas. Today, it is certainly the **most important law-making procedure**.

? 3.8 Briefly outline other legislative procedures of the EC

In a number of cases, relating to the fixing of the Community's common customs tariff (Article 26 TEC) (→ *7.1, 11.2*), capital restrictions (Articles 57 and 59 TEC), the Common Commercial Policy (Article 133 TEC) (→ *11.1, 11.2*), sanctions against non-EU states (Article 301 TEC) (→ *11.22*) and others, the Treaty provides for the **Council** acting on a proposal by the

Commission **without EP input**. In practice, however, the EP is often voluntarily consulted.

Very exceptionally, the **Commission** may legislate on its own. Article 86(3) TEC gives the Commission alone the power to adopt directives and decisions concerning public undertakings ($\rightarrow 9.32$).

According to the so-called **assent procedure** the Council acts on obtaining the assent of the EP. Parliament's approval requires an absolute majority of the votes cast (or absolute majority of its members for accession ($\rightarrow 1.7$) and the uniform electoral procedure). The assent procedure was introduced by the 1986 SEA for important matters, such as accession and association agreements ($\rightarrow 11.3$), and now also applies to certain tasks of the European Central Bank and the structural funds (such as the European Agricultural Guidance and Guarantee Fund or the European Regional Development Fund) as well as the Cohesion Fund.

? 3.9 Explain the choice of legislative procedures if more than one legal basis is available to Community institutions

By selecting a particular legal basis for Community legislation, the EU institutions may try to avoid 'problems' either in the Council, for example, by using a procedure requiring QMV instead of unanimity, or in the Parliament, for example, by opting for a procedure where Parliament has less influence than in co-decision. In order to prevent such **'procedure shopping'**, the ECJ has exercised its annulment power ($\rightarrow 5.8$).

According to settled ECJ case law, as expressed in the *Indirect Tax Recovery* Case, Case C-388/01 *Commission* v. *Council* [2004] ECR I-4829, 'the choice of the legal basis for a Community measure must rest on objective factors amenable to judicial review, which include in particular the aim and the content of the measure'. Where the Court is able to identify a primary purpose and content of Community legislation, 'the act must be based on a single legal basis, namely that required by the main or predominant purpose or component'.

The ECJ's search for the **primary purpose** of Community legislation in order to determine its legal basis has already been pursued in the so-called *Waste Directive* Case. In Case C-155/91 *Commission* v. *Council* [1993] ECR I-939, the Court stipulated that the 'nature, aim and context of the act in question' should be analysed. In the Court's view the main focus of the directive was environmental, implementing such ecological principles as rectification at source and waste transport minimisation, and not the internal market principle of free movement of waste. It, thus, found that the environmental basis for legislation under Article 130s (now Article 175) TEC was correct and prevailed over the internal market basis of Article 100a (now Article 95) TEC.

Where it is not possible to identify a primary purpose and content of Community legislation, the ECJ will apply a hierarchical test, establishing which of the Treaty articles serving as possible legal basis prevails over the other. The use of this different test can be seen in the *Titanium Dioxide* Case, and it explains why the outcome was different. Case C-300/89 *Commission* v. *Council* [1991] ECR 1991 I-2867, concerned the use of the correct legislative procedure by the Community's institutions, in particular, whether a directive, that is, Council Directive 89/428/EEC of 21 June 1989 on procedures for harmonising the programmes for the reduction and eventual elimination of pollution caused by waste from the titanium dioxide industry, was to be adopted in accordance with Article 100a TEC (calling for the co-operation procedure) or according to Article 130s TEC (providing for unanimity and EP consultation). The ECJ annulled the 1989 directive which had been adopted unanimously by the Council on the basis of Article 130s (now Article 175) TEC. While acknowledging that both provisions could serve as the legal basis for the Community act in question, the Court held that the 'use of both provisions as a joint legal basis would divest the cooperation procedure of its very substance' and that it was thus necessary to determine the appropriate legal basis. The ECJ held that this would have been Article 100a (now Article 95) TEC calling for the co-operation procedure and thus a larger role of EP. In the Court's view the internal market harmonisation power under Article 100a TEC could pursue environmental purposes and was thus hierarchically superior to Article 130s TEC.

3.10 What does the notion of 'democratic deficit' stand for?

Since the 1990s the debate about the **democratic legitimacy** of the EU has focused on a number of actual and perceived deficiencies, mostly under the concept of 'democratic deficit'. It stands for a lack of direct democratic law-making as a result of less than fully representative decision making, for a 'bypassing of democracy' through **comitology** (→ *2.15*) and other legislative techniques where the executive dominates, and for the 'transparency and complexity issue' resulting from Council voting behind closed doors, etc.

One of the possible answers to the lack of direct democratic legitimacy is usually found in the 'indirect legitimacy' through representatives of the Member States in the Council. These are government officials who are selected on the basis of a democratic consensus in the Member States. At the same time, the increased role of the EP, whose members have been directly elected since 1979 (→ *2.16*), may equally counterweight the present 'democratic deficit'.

4 The effect of Community law

Community law, that is, the treaties and secondary law made according to the different legislative procedures, is directly applied and enforced by EU institutions only exceptionally. The most important exception relates to the Commission's power to enforce EC competition law (Articles 81 and 82 TEC, as well as Regulation 17, now Regulation 1/2003). In addition, the Commission also exercises other treaty-based or delegated powers.

Most Community law, however, is applied and enforced in a decentralised fashion by national authorities. As a rule, the courts and administrative agencies of the Member States apply and enforce 'directly applicable' EC law as well as nationally implemented non-directly applicable Community law.

This chapter will explain how the European Court of Justice has made Community law ever more effective by declaring not only regulations, but also Treaty provisions and provisions in directives – under certain circumstances – directly applicable/effective in the legal systems of the Member States.

4.1 What do we understand by 'direct effect'?

A norm of international or supranational law is said to have 'direct effect' if it is sufficiently clear, precise and unconditional to be invoked before national courts or administrative agencies.

In EC law 'direct effect' may attach to provisions of the Treaty, of international agreements of the Community and secondary legislation, including, under certain circumstances, even to directives.

As opposed to **general international law**, where states are considered to be **free** as to **how** they **implement** international obligations and where direct effect, thus, normally depends upon national constitutional law governing the 'incorporation' of international law into the national legal order, the ECJ developed case law according to which the **direct effect** of **Community law is an inherent characteristic** of, and required by, EC law. The Court has already stated in the famous *Van Gend* Case, Case 26/62 *Van Gend en Loos* v. *Nederlandse Administratie der Belastingen* [1963] ECR 1 (→ *1.5, 4.4*), that:

> independently of the legislation of Member States, Community law therefore not only imposes obligations on individuals but is also intended to confer upon them rights which become part of their legal heritage.

4.2 What is the difference between 'direct applicability' and 'direct effect'?

To a large extent these two terms are used **interchangeably**. Even early ECJ cases such as *Van Gend* used them synonymously. There is one distinction that may be derived directly from the text of the EC Treaty. While Article 249 TEC (→ *ch. 3*) states that regulations are 'directly applicable in all Member States', the Treaty does not use the term 'direct effect' at all. It also does not provide for the 'direct applicability' of certain Treaty norms or rules contained in directives. Therefore, 'direct effect' can be seen as a substitute for a largely similar concept.

In a number of ECJ cases, 'direct effect' is used when emphasising that rights are conferred upon **individuals**; it thus mainly implies that individuals can rely upon or **invoke** a norm having direct effect before national courts and tribunals.

4.3 What is the rationale for 'direct effect'?

The major policy rationale behind 'direct effect' of Community law norms lies in the fact that this strongly enhances the effectiveness (*'effet utile'*) and **uniform application** of EC law, and thereby contributes to the ideal of legal integration by creating a homogeneous legal order in which all market participants enjoy the same legal rights and obligations. According to Case 26/62 *Van Gend en Loos* v. *Nederlandse Administratie der Belastingen* [1963] ECR 1 (→ *4.4*), the Treaty implies 'more than mutual obligations of States, also their nationals are subjects of this new legal order'.

A further, more technical justification for 'direct effect' stems from the procedural devices available under the TEC. Article 234 TEC, which enables national courts to refer questions concerning the validity and interpretation of EC law to the ECJ (→ *5.14–19*), somehow presupposes the direct relevance of EC law in private party suits before national courts. Direct effect thus makes **'decentralised law enforcement'** possible, and thereby adds to the traditional international control of Treaty compliance by actions brought against Member States by the Commission or by other Member States according to Articles 226 and 227 TEC (→ *5.11, 5.12*).

4.4 Can Treaty provisions have direct effect?

The most important 'objective' requirement for 'direct effect' seems to be that the norm in question has to be sufficiently 'clear, precise and unconditional' (→ *4.1*). In its case law the ECJ has accorded **direct effect** to a number of **TEC provisions** and clarified the meaning of the direct applicability of regulations and decisions.

The first case establishing that Treaty provisions may have direct effect was the famous *Van Gend* Case, Case 26/62 *Van Gend en Loos* v. *Nederlandse Administratie der Belastingen* [1963] ECR 1. It involved a Dutch importer who claimed that he was charged an increased import duty on products from Germany contrary to Article 12 (now Article 25) TEC (→ *7.2*). The Court interpreted the obligation under this article not to impose any new or higher import duties as a 'clear and unconditional . . . negative obligation . . . ideally adapted to produce direct effects in the legal relationships between Member States and their subjects'. Going beyond the wording of Article 12 TEC, the Court also found that Article 12 applied and explained one of the 'essential provisions' of the Treaty, that is, the prohibition of customs duties and charges having equivalent effect. It considered this to be relevant with regard to the **general scheme** of the EC Treaty. Lastly, with regard to the **'spirit'** of the Treaty, the ECJ noted that its **objective** to establish a Common Market (→ *7.1*) 'implies that this Treaty is more than an agreement which merely creates mutual obligations between the contracting states'. Rather, the Court held that 'the Community constitutes a new legal order of international law for the benefit of which the states have limited their sovereign rights, albeit within limited fields, and the subjects of which comprise not only Member States but also their nationals'. Thus, the Court concluded that 'according to the spirit, the general scheme and the wording of the Treaty, Article 12 must be interpreted as producing direct effects and creating individual rights which national courts must protect'.

4.5 Are there any limits to the potential direct effect of TEC provisions?

In subsequent cases also 'positive obligations' were clearly held to produce 'direct effect'. The required standard of 'clear, precise and unconditional' has been interpreted rather liberally in a number of far-reaching decisions by the ECJ. For instance, in Case 2/74 *Reyners* v. *Belgium* [1974] ECR 631, involving a clear discrimination on the basis of nationality, the Court declared that Article 52 (now Article 43) TEC had direct effect and could be relied upon by an individual so discriminated against ($\rightarrow$ *8.12, 8.13*). This was remarkable because Article 52 TEC, at that time, provided for the abolition of restrictions on the **freedom of establishment** of Community nationals in states other than that of their nationality 'within the framework of the provisions set out below'. The relevant 'framework' included a general programme and a number of directives which, contrary to the intentions of the Treaty, had not been adopted after the transitional period as planned. Still, the Court held that 'after the expiry of the transitory period the directive provided for by the Chapter on the right of establishment have become superfluous with regard to implementing the rule on nationality, since this is henceforth sanctioned by the Treaty itself with direct effect'.

In Case 43/75 *Defrenne* v. *Sabena* [1976] ECR 455, which can be regarded as an outstanding example of **teleological interpretation** guided by the *effet utile* of Community law, the Court considered the principle of **equal pay** to be **directly effective** ($\rightarrow$ *5.10, 10.17*). This was remarkable since the text of what was then Article 119 (now the amended Article 141) TEC clearly was not very precise. Article 119(1) TEC provided as follows: 'Each Member State shall during the first stage ensure and subsequently maintain the application of the principle that men and women should receive equal pay for equal work.' Nevertheless, the ECJ found that the plaintiff could rely upon this provision against her employer before Belgian courts.

The limits as to the **objective requirements** of clarity and precision (→ *4.1*) can be seen in Case 126/86 *Zaera* v. *Institutio Nacionale de la Seguridad Social* [1987] ECR 3697, a case in which a Spanish national wanted to rely on Article 2 TEC in order to challenge a Spanish social security incompatibility provision prohibiting him from becoming a civil servant while receiving a retirement pension. Article 2 TEC provides, among other things, that 'the Community shall have as its task . . . an accelerated raising of the standard of living'. In rejecting the claim, the ECJ reasoned that the accelerated raising of the standard of living was one of the aims of the EC, which 'owing to its general terms and its systematic dependence on the establishment of the Common Market and progressive approximation of economic policies, cannot impose legal obligations on Member States or confer rights on individuals'.

4.6 What are the pre-conditions for a norm of secondary Community law to have direct effect?

Although **regulations** are by definition 'directly applicable in all Member States' they may, in **exceptional** cases, require **implementing measures** by the Member States if their provisions are not sufficiently clear and precise or, more likely, if they expressly provide for such implementing measures. In Case 50/76 *Amsterdam Bulb BV* [1977] ECR 137, the ECJ has warned Member States, however, that with regard to directly applicable regulations they may not 'adopt any measure which would conceal the Community nature and effects of any legal provision from the person to whom it applies'; for instance, by enacting implementing legislation in a somewhat different form.

The Treaty does not say anything about the direct applicability of **decisions**. Article 249 TEC merely states that a decision is 'binding in its entirety upon those to whom it is addressed'. The question that arose in litigation before German courts was whether individuals could rely upon Council decisions addressed to the Member States which related to the VAT directive. In a preliminary ruling (→ *5.14*), Case 9/70 *Franz Grad* v. *Finanzamt Traunstein* [1970] ECR 838, the ECJ reasoned that in cases where:

> the Community authorities by means of a decision have imposed an obligation on a Member State or all the Member States to act in a certain way, the effectiveness (*l'effet utile*) of such a measure would be weakened if the nationals of that State could not invoke it in the courts and the national courts would not take it into consideration as part of Community law.

❓ 4.7 Are directives 'directly effective'?

As a matter of principle, **directives** are **not directly applicable** or effective. Article 249 TEC provides that they 'shall be binding as to the result to be achieved, upon each Member State to which it is addressed, but shall leave to the national authorities the choice of form and methods'. As a primary tool for legal **harmonisation** (→ *3.5*) they are intended to lead to an 'approximation of the law', not to absolute unification, as do regulations. By leaving the choice of implementation to the Member States, directives are a **means of federalism**. Serious problems do arise, however, if Member States refuse or fail to implement properly. The effectiveness of Community law would clearly suffer under such conditions. Thus, inspired by its *effet utile* approach, the ECJ has developed a jurisprudence according to which even provisions of directives may exceptionally be considered directly effective.

The leading case is Case 41/74 *Van Duyn* v. *Home Office* [1974] ECR 1337, in which a Dutch national was refused entry into the UK because she intended to work for the Church of Scientology, which was officially regarded as socially harmful. The Court held that she could rely on a provision of Directive 64/221, which required that public policy measures had to be based on the personal conduct of the individual concerned (→ 8.9).

Direct effect may work both as a **'shield'** and a **'sword'**. In the *Ratti* Case, Case 148/78 *Ministerio Pubblico* v. *Ratti* [1979] ECR 1629, it protected an Italian national who had complied with the labelling provisions of two directives which had not been implemented in time by the Italian legislator against criminal prosecution under the more stringent Italian rules. The court held that 'a Member State which has not adopted the implementing measures required by the directive in the prescribed periods may not rely, as against individuals, on its own failure to perform the obligations which the directive entails'. It thereby provided an important policy rationale for the direct effect of directives, the **estoppel** reasoning, that is, Member States should be precluded from relying on their failure to implement directives correctly.

In Case 8/81 *Becker* v. *Finanzamt Münster-Innenstadt* [1982] ECR 53, direct effect was used as a 'sword' by allowing a German taxpayer to calculate her tax returns in accordance with unimplemented provisions of Community directives.

The present law on direct effect of directives may be restated as follows: wherever **provisions** of a **directive** are **unconditional and sufficiently precise** and **in the absence of implementing measures** adopted **within the prescribed period**, they can be **directly relied upon**, even against any national provision which is incompatible with the directive. This latter aspect is discussed below under the heading of **supremacy** (→ *4.10, 4.11*) of EC law.

? 4.8 What is 'horizontal' direct effect?

The cases starting with *Van Duyn* (→ *4.7*) concerned individuals who were able to rely upon EC directives vis-à-vis Member States which had failed to implement them (so-called **vertical direct effect**). At some stage the question arose as to whether such direct effect could also take place vis-à-vis private individuals, that is, **horizontally**.

Clearly, this would enhance the effectiveness of Community law (*effet utile*). However, since the leading case of *Marshall*, Case 152/84 *Marshall* v. *Southampton and South-West Hampshire Area Health Authority (Teaching)* [1986] ECR 723 (→ *10.23*), the ECJ has consistently **refused** to permit a **horizontal direct effect** for **directives** as a matter of principle. Based on the wording of Article 249 TEC, the Court has argued that a directive was binding only upon 'each Member State to which it is addressed. It follows that such a directive may not of itself impose obligations on an individual and that a provision of a directive may not be relied upon as such against such a person.' The advocate-general's opinion (→ *5.2*) added two further concerns militating against 'horizontal' direct effect. First, it would have eliminated the **difference** between **regulations and directives**; and secondly, since directives were not published in the Official Journal, which was the case until the entry into force of the TEU (→ *1.8*), the private party against which it might be relied upon may not even have had notice of it. One may add that 'horizontal' direct effect would be difficult to reconcile with another main justification for direct effect next to the estoppel argument (→ *4.7*), the rationale of punishing a defaulting

Member State. Why should private parties be blamed for the failure of states to implement directives?

In order to mitigate the limiting result of denying 'horizontal' direct effect, the ECJ has developed a number of judicial techniques expanding the effect of direct effect.

Starting with the *Marshall* Case, the Court has relied on a broad concept of the state which includes the state in its 'private capacity' as an employer. Summarising its own case law, the ECJ noted in Case C-188/89 *Foster* v. *British Gas* [1990] ECR I-3313, that directives could be relied upon against tax authorities, local or regional authorities, constitutionally independent authorities responsible for the maintenance of public order and safety and public authorities providing public health services. It then concluded:

> It follows from the foregoing that a body, whatever its legal form, which has been made responsible, pursuant to a measure adopted by the State, for providing a public service under the control of the State and has for that purpose special powers beyond those which result from the normal rules applicable in relations between individuals, is included in any event among the bodies against which the provisions of a directive capable of having direct effect may be relied upon.

An alternative avenue was opened up by the Court's development of an 'indirect (horizontal) effect' of directives. According to this interpretation maxim, national law has to be interpreted in the light of directives. It was expressly used in Case 106/89 *Marleasing SA* v. *La Comercial* [1990] ECR I-4135, in which the plaintiff company sought a declaratory judgment invalidating the contract of incorporation of another Spanish company that had been procured by misrepresentation and fraud to the detriment of its creditors, one of whom was Marleasing. Spanish law provided for such a remedy, whereas the defendant claimed that the exhaustive list of a non-implemented Council directive, which did not include such a remedy for misrepresentation and fraud, would exclude Marleasing's claim. In a preliminary ruling the ECJ denied horizontal direct effect, but held that:

> a national court called upon to interpret [national law] is required to do so, as far as possible in the light of the wording and the purpose of the Directive in order to achieve a result pursued by the latter and thereby comply with the third paragraph of Article [249 TEC].

The Court has set some limits to the principle of 'indirect effect' of directives, although some of the more recent cases blur the line between mere 'indirect effect' and 'horizontal' direct effect. In Case 80/86 *Kolpinghuis Nijmegen* [1987] ECR 3969, the Court held that 'a directive cannot, of itself and independently of a law adopted for its implementation, have the effect of determining or aggravating the liability in criminal law of persons who act in contravention of the provision of that directive'.

Horizontal direct effect is, however, recognised for **Treaty provisions** (→ *4.4, 4.5, 8.5*). This was confirmed in Case 43/75 *Defrenne* v. *Sabena* [1976] ECR 455, for Article 119 (now Article 141) TEC (→ *4.4, 10.17*). It is also clear for the Treaty rules on competition in Articles 81 and 82 TEC (→*ch. 9*). In Case C-281/93 *Angonese* [2000] ECR I-4134, it was also found to apply to Article 39 TEC concerning the free movement of workers (→*8.5*).

? 4.9 Are there any remedies if directives are not 'directly effective'?

In the *Francovich* case, Joined Cases C-6/90 and C-9/90 *Francovich and Bonifaci* v. *Italian Republic* [1991] ECR I-5357, the ECJ held that the principle of **responsibility** of the state for **damages** caused to individuals by the state's **violations** of **Community law** is **'inherent in the Treaty system'** and can be based on Article 5 TEC. Under Article 5 TEC they are required to take all appropriate measures, whether general or particular, to ensure the implementation of Community law, and consequently to nullify the unlawful consequences of a breach of Community law. The plaintiffs had instituted proceedings seeking damages from the Italian state for failure to implement Directive 80/987 on the protection of employees in the event of the insolvency of the employer (→ *10.15*). Their employer had become insolvent and since there were no Italian implementing measures the plaintiffs did not receive any wage payments guaranteed under the directive. The Court held that the directive was **not directly effective** because the obligor under the system of salary protection in case of insolvency was **not clearly determined**. However, the Court enunciated the **principle of state liability** for failure to implement a directive for which it basically set three conditions:

(1) the result prescribed by the directive involves the **grant of rights to individuals**;
(2) the **content** of these rights is **identifiable**; and
(3) there is a **causal link** between the violation of EC law, the non-implementation of the directive, and the damage suffered by individuals.

The Court added that the jurisdiction and procedure for such damage claims are left to the law of the Member States which has to provide **an effective remedy**.

In Joined Cases C-24/93 and C-48/93 *Brasserie du Pêcheur/Factortame III* [1996] ECR I-1029, a follow-up to the *German Beer* Case (→ *7.8*), the ECJ clarified a number of conceptual issues concerning state liability. It held that compensation was also available in case of breaches of directly effective EC law, such as the free movement of goods (→ *ch. 7*) or the freedom of establishment (→ *ch. 8*). It further held that state liability could be derived not only from Article 5 (now Article 10) TEC, but was also a 'general principle familiar to the legal systems of the member states that an unlawful act or omission gives rise to an obligation to make good the damage caused' – a general principle which also found its expression in Article 215 (now Article 288) TEC providing for the non-contractual liability of the Community (→ *10.5*). On the basis of an analogy to the requirements for Community liability under Article 288 TEC, the Court slightly modified the requirements set out in the *Francovich* Case for the non-implementation of directives to the following more broadly applicable rule:

> Community law confers a right to reparation where three conditions are met: the rule of law infringed must be intended to confer rights on individuals; the breach must be sufficiently serious; and there must be a direct causal link between the breach of the obligation resting on the State and the damage sustained by the injured party.

In Case C-224/01 *Köbler* v. *Austria* [2003] ECR I-10239, the ECJ held that the *Francovich* principle also applied to acts of the judiciary, such as a breach of the Article 234(3) TEC obligation to make a reference to the ECJ (→ *5.16, 5.19*).

4.10 Explain the significance of the case of Costa v. ENEL

Mr Costa, shareholder of an electricity company which was nationalised by Italy, was billed for electricity by the national electricity company ENEL. Since he refused to pay his bill he was sued by ENEL. In the national court proceedings, Mr Costa raised as a defence that the nationalisation was contrary

to EC law. Though Community law does not prohibit expro-
priations because it expressly leaves issues concerning property
rights outside the scope of the TEC, the ECJ in Case 6/64
Flaminio Costa v. *ENEL* [1964] ECR 585, held that Article 37
(now Article 31) TEC, prohibiting the introduction of any new
state monopolies of a commercial character, was directly effective and prohibited the Italian nationalisation measures. The
matter was, however, a little more complicated since the Italian
nationalisation legislation was adopted after the conclusion of
the EC Treaty, and according to Italian constitutional law the
norm later in time (*lex posterior*) would prevail over the earlier
one. Reiterating its reasoning in the *Van Gend* Case (→ *4.4*),
the ECJ nevertheless insisted that Community law stands for
an autonomous legal order which by itself required not only
direct effect but also – in case of conflict between a directly
applicable Community norm and a norm of the national legal
order – the 'supremacy' or 'primacy' of EC law. According to
the court:

> the integration into the laws of each Member State of
> provisions which derive from the Community, and more
> generally the terms and the spirit of the Treaty, make
> it impossible for the States, as a corollary, to accord
> precedence to a unilateral and subsequent measure over
> a legal system accepted by them on a basis of reciprocity.

It is clear that the *effet utile* has found victory again: the
supremacy of EC law over national law enhances the legal uniformity and effectiveness of EC law.

In later cases, such as Case 11/79 *Internationale
Handelsgesellschaft* [1970] ECR 1125, the ECJ clarified the
meaning of the *Costa* judgment and held that the supremacy
of EC law also applied vis-à-vis national constitutional law (→
6.6, 6.9).

4.11   What are the Simmenthal cases?

The impact of a conflict between national constitutional law and Community law came to a head in the *Simmenthal* Case, where it was a rather unimportant piece of secondary Community law that collided with Italian constitutional law.

The first *Simmenthal* Case, Case 35/76 *Simmenthal SpA* v. *Ministero dello Finanze* [1976] ECR 1871, was a preliminary ruling in 1976 in which the ECJ held that Italian **charges** for veterinary and health inspections of imported beef were effectively **equivalent to customs duties** and thus contrary to the free movement of goods (→ *7.2*).

Simmenthal II, Case 106/77 *Amministrazione delle Finanze dello Stato* v. *Simmenthal SpA* [1978] ECR 629, was a follow-up preliminary ruling concerning an Italian court ordering the fiscal authorities to **repay the illegal charges** to the importer. In these proceedings the Italian Ministry of Finance argued that according to Italian law only the Italian Constitutional Court could invalidate an Italian law (on which the charges were based) conflicting with higher norms (the EEC Treaty). The Italian court again referred the case to the ECJ, asking whether the national law must be immediately disregarded or not. The ECJ reiterated the principle of **primacy** of EC law and deduced from it the rule that 'every national court must, in a case within its jurisdiction, apply Community law in its entirety and protect rights which the latter confers upon individuals and must set aside any provision of national law which may conflict with it, whether prior or subsequent to the Community rule'. Thus, in the view of the ECJ it was 'not necessary to request or await the prior setting aside of such provision by legislative or other constitutional means'.

4.12 May international agreements produce direct effect?

The question of the direct effect of **international agreements** (→ *11.3*) relates not only to their status within the legal order of the Member States but also to the Community legal order, in particular whether they may be invoked before the ECJ.

With regard to **free trade agreements** (→ *7.1*, *11.3*) concluded by the Community with third countries, the ECJ held in the *Kupferberg* Case, Case 104/81 *Hauptzollamt Mainz* v. *Kupferberg* [1982] ECR 3641, that certain provisions of the EC–Portugal Free Trade Agreement (before Portugal joined the Community) did have **direct effect**, because they were sufficiently precise, unconditional and their direct application was within the purpose of the agreement. This ruling immediately followed a diametrically opposed outcome in the *Polydor* Case, Case 270/80 *Polydor Ltd & RSO Records Inc.* v. *Harlequin Record Shops Ltd and others* [1982] ECR 329, wherein the ECJ had held that another provision of the same free trade agreement – though identically worded to a directly applicable TEC provision – should not be given direct effect since the free trade agreement and the TEC had different aims and purposes.

The ECJ has meanwhile given direct effect to a number of provisions contained in **association and cooperation agreements** (→ *11.3*, *11.11*), and more recently also to the provisions on freedom of establishment of some **Europe agreements** (→ *1.7*, *11.13*) with Eastern European countries. In Case C-192/89 *Sevince* v. *Staatssecretaris Van Justitie* [1990] ECR I-3461, even the secondary legislation of such agreements, such as **decisions** adopted by **association councils** (→ *11.11*), has been regarded as amenable to **direct effect**.

? 4.13 May an individual claim that EC legislation is in violation of GATT/WTO principles?

Contrary to its case law on free trade agreements and despite quite a lot of criticism, the ECJ has consistently refused to consider GATT provisions directly applicable.

The leading case is Case 21-24/72 *International Fruit Company* v. *Produktschap voor Groenten en Fruit* [1972] ECR 1219 (→ *11.10*), in which an apple importer's import licence was rejected by Dutch customs authorities on the basis of EC regulations which were arguably in violation of Article XI GATT. The ECJ rejected the direct effect of this provision, holding that the GATT did not confer rights on citizens of the Community on which they could rely before the courts. The Court invoked the 'great flexibility' of the GATT's provisions, the possibility of derogation from its obligations, the option of measures in exceptional difficulties and the peculiar GATT conflict settlement provisions, such as unilateral suspension rights, as reasons preventing the direct effect of the GATT.

This negative attitude towards the GATT was reaffirmed in one of the many *Banana* cases before the ECJ. In Case 280/93 *Germany* v. *Commission* [1994] ECR I-4873, the Court held that 'GATT rules are not unconditional . . . an obligation to recognize them as rules of international law which are directly applicable in the domestic legal systems of the contracting parties cannot be based on the spirit, general scheme or terms of GATT'. One of the main reasons why the GATT provisions were considered not to be unconditional was that the GATT did contain numerous exceptions, had only a rather weak dispute settlement system and always provided the opportunity for 'losing' parties to offer compensation instead of complying with the recommendations of a GATT panel ruling. With the new dispute settlement provisions of the WTO after the Uruguay

Round, which also implied a 'juridification' of the trade diplomacy of the GATT, many observers expected a change of attitude on the part of the ECJ. This expectation was, however, disappointed in Case C-149/96 *Portugal* v. *Council* [1999] ECR I-8395, in which the ECJ found that 'WTO agreements are not in principle among the rules in the light of which the Court is to review the legality of measures adopted by the Community institutions'. The Court reasoned that even under the 1994 WTO Dispute Settlement Understanding the parties still had broad opportunities for negotiations. Probably most important, the Court noted that the lack of reciprocity with regard to the willingness to directly apply GATT law might lead to serious imbalances which would deprive the Community of the possibility of negotiating trade compensation instead of complying with the strict terms of the WTO agreements.

In practice, the **denial of direct effect** has been somewhat **mitigated** in two types of situations in which the Court has held that GATT provisions may be invoked in order to claim an incompatibility of EC legislation. In accordance with ECJ case law, the Court may thus review the GATT legality of Community acts (a) if the Community **intended to implement** a particular GATT obligation (Case C-69/89 *Nakajima* [1991] ECR 2069), or (b) if the Community act **expressly referred to** specific GATT provisions (Case 70/87 *Fediol* [1994] ECR I-4873).

5 Judicial control within the Community

To a considerable degree EC law has been shaped by the **European Court of Justice (ECJ)**. The Court has rightly been called a **'motor of integration'** because, in the years of Euro-scepticism and political standstill on the question of 'deepening' the Community, it has largely created the *'acquis communautaire'*. Its case law, in particular in the field of the **four freedoms**, has made a significant contribution to the harmonisation and mutual recognition of national standards which, in turn, was essential for the creation of a true **internal market**.

The Court was able to attain this crucial role as a **'quasi-lawmaker'** because of its broad jurisdictional powers. In fact, the ECJ acts as **'constitutional court'** of the EU exercising **'judicial review'** over both the EU/EC and its Member States. According to the ECJ's own reasoning in Case 294/83 *Les Verts* v. *Parliament* [1986] ECR 1356, the Community is:

> based on the rule of law, inasmuch as neither its Member States nor its institutions can avoid a review of whether measures adopted by them are in conformity with the basic constitutional charter, the Treaty. The Treaty established the Court as the judicial body responsible for ensuring that both the Member States and the Community institutions comply with the law.

The ECJ, composed of judges from all Member States, exercises this judicial control mainly through **'annulment actions'** directed against acts of the EU institutions, 'infringement actions' directed against Member States and 'preliminary rulings' providing guidance to national courts for the interpretation of Community law.

The following section will demonstrate that the ECJ's jurisdictional powers go far beyond the usual dispute settlement mechanisms provided for in international organisations, by explaining in some detail the Court's powers of judicial control after a brief overview of its institutional structure.

? 5.1 Who sits on the European Court of Justice?

According to Article 223 TEC, the 'Judges and Advocates-General of the Court of Justice shall be chosen from persons whose independence is beyond doubt and who possess the qualifications required for appointment to the highest judicial offices in their respective countries or who are jurisconsults of recognised competence.' The ECJ, seated in Luxembourg, is currently composed of twenty-seven judges (one 'nominated' by each Member State) and eight advocates-general. They are appointed by common accord of the governments of the Member States for a renewable term of six years. A registrar, who is among other things responsible for the Court's administration and for the publication of its decisions, is elected by the judges. Judges and advocates-general each have three 'legal secretaries' who perform the tasks of law clerks. Today, the Court sits in plenary session (as a 'full court') only very rarely in cases of 'exceptional importance' or in a number of impeachment-like procedures aimed at depriving senior Community officials of their office. Equally rare are cases decided by a so-called Grand Chamber of thirteen judges, which will be convened on the request of a Member State or a Community institution as a party to legal proceedings. Normally, the Court will hear cases in **chambers** of three or **five judges**.

Though all Community languages are used in legal proceedings before the Court, its **working language** remains **French**. The ECJ is in permanent session and has delivered several thousand decisions since 1954.

? 5.2 What is the task of an advocate-general?

According to Article 222 TEC, it is for the **advocates-general**, 'acting with complete **impartiality** and **independence**, to make, in open court, **reasoned submissions**'. The position of an advocate-general was inspired by the 'commissaire du gouvernement' of the French Conseil d'Etat. It could be viewed as an institutionalised *'amicus curiae'* (literally a 'friend of the court'), whose opinions, although not binding, are in most cases followed by the Court and published as annexes to ECJ judgments.

? 5.3 Describe the scope of jurisdiction of the Court of First Instance and the Civil Service Tribunal

As provided for in the 1986 SEA, a **Court of First Instance** (CFI) was established by a Council Decision in 1988 and started functioning in 1989. It currently consists of twenty-seven judges, but the TEC provides that there could be more than one judge per Member State. The CFI usually sits in chambers of three or five judges, though its rules of procedure provide that 'whenever the legal difficulty or the importance of the case or special circumstances so justify' it may decide as a Grand Chamber or as a full court. Since 1999 even single judges may decide routine cases.

One of the main purposes of setting up the CFI was to reduce the case-load of the ECJ. This concern shaped the scope of the CFI's jurisdiction. Originally, the CFI was competent for staff and competition law cases (→ 9.15), as well as for cases brought by individuals under the ECSC Treaty. The CFI's jurisdiction was broadened by a number of amendments to now include basically all direct actions by private parties. Preliminary rulings are still excluded from the CFI's jurisdiction, although there is a provision in the TEC after the Nice Treaty (→ 5.14) that would allow the transfer of this jurisdiction to the CFI. When it became evident that the case-load for the two Community courts remained at very high levels, another 'outsourcing' of judicial tasks was decided upon. On the basis of a provision in the Nice Treaty, the Council decided in 2004 to establish a European Union Civil Service Tribunal consisting of seven judges competent to hear staff disputes between the Communities and their employees.

Appeals against a CFI decision are possible within two months on questions of law. The ECJ may then give final judgment itself or refer the matter back to the CFI.

5.4 What are the main types of procedures before the ECJ?

Although the Court's task is broadly defined as to ensure that 'the law is observed' in the interpretation and application of the Treaty, the principle of enumerated powers (→3.1), valid for all Community institutions, also implies that the ECJ has jurisdiction only for the specific types of procedures mentioned in the Treaty. The three most important procedures are:

(1) the action for annulment according to Article 230 TEC (→ 5.5–10) (which is complemented by the complaint of failure to act according to Article 232 TEC in cases where there is no Community act in place);

(2) **infringement proceedings** against Member States according to Articles 226, 227 and 228 TEC (→ *5.11–13*); and
(3) **preliminary references** according to Article 234 TEC (→
5.14–19).

5.5 What kind of 'acts' may be reviewed under an Article 230 TEC action for annulment?

Community **legislation**, typically regulations, directives and
decisions (→ *ch. 3*), are **subject to annulment** proceedings. The
ECJ clarified early on that the precise form of Community acts
is immaterial. In Case 60/81 *IBM* v. *Commission* [1981] ECR
2639, it held that 'any measure the legal effects of which are
binding on, and capable of affecting the interests of, the applicant by bringing about a distinct change in his legal position is
an act . . . under Article [230]'. In that case, a Commission letter
which only informed IBM that competition law proceedings
(→ *ch. 9*) had been instituted against it was held not to be open
to challenge under Article 230 TEC.

In the so-called *ERTA* Case, Case 22/70 *Commission* v.
Council [1971] ECR 263, the ECJ held that 'an action for annulment must be available in the case of all measures adopted
by the institutions, whatever their nature or form, which are
intended to have legal effect'. The Court found that a Council
'resolution', adopting a negotiating procedure, 'had definitive
legal effects both on relations between the Community and the
Member States and on the relationship between the institutions'
and was thus **reviewable**.

5.6 Can an individual also bring annulment actions?

Member States, the **Commission**, the **Council** and – since the
Nice Treaty – also the **Parliament**, the so-called **privileged**

applicants, have an unconditional **right** to ask the Court to **review the legality** of Community acts. The Court of Auditors and the European Central Bank can do so for the protection of their prerogatives.

Natural or **legal persons**, however, have to prove their **special legal interest** in order to have **standing** or, as lawyers tend to say, *locus standi*, to seek judicial review. In the terms of the TEC, this will be the case if it concerns a 'decision addressed to that **person'** – as is regularly the case in **competition** law decisions ($\rightarrow$ *ch. 9*) – or when it involves a 'decision, which, although in the form of a **regulation** or a decision addressed to another person, is of **direct and individual concern** to the former'. These standing requirements enshrined in Article 230(4) TEC have given rise to a considerable body of case law by the ECJ, which has not always been very encouraging for individual applicants.

In fact, by laying down rather **restrictive** criteria in the early *Plaumann* Case, Case 25/62 *Plaumann & Co.* v. *Commission* [1963] ECR 95, from which the Court has not since distanced itself, the ECJ has considerably reduced the number of review cases brought by individual plaintiffs. In that case the Court held that:

> persons other than those to whom a decision is addressed may only claim to be individually concerned if that decision affects them by reason of certain attributes which are peculiar to them or by reason of circumstances in which they are differentiated from all other persons and by virtue of these factors distinguishes them individually just as in the case of the person addressed.

One of the **rare cases** where this standard was met was the *Töpfer* Case, Cases 106 and 107/63 *Alfred Töpfer and Getreide-Import Gesellschaft* v. *Commission* [1965] ECR 405. In that case, a Commission decision addressed to Germany authorising it to reject import licences as a safeguard measure was considered to be of individual concern to importers, because the only persons affected by the said measures were the importers who had already applied for a licence. The number and identity of these importers had already become fixed and ascertainable before the date when the contested decision was made.

Individual challenges to decisions addressed to other persons occur most frequently in disputes concerning state aid ($\rightarrow$ 9.33). Thus, Commission decisions which deny Member States the right to grant subsidies are regularly challenged by the potential recipients of such aid.

Under the *Plaumann* test individual challenges to regulations are almost always excluded. An exception can be seen in Case C-309/89 *Codorniu SA* v. *Council* [1994] ECR I-1853. There, the Court accepted that the Spanish sparkling wine producer and trademark owner of 'Gran Crémant' could challenge a Council regulation reserving the term 'crémant' to French and Luxembourg sparkling wines, because this regulation was of individual concern to the applicant.

In practice, the most frequent cases of successful individual challenges to regulations are found in the area of anti-dumping law ($\rightarrow$ 11.2). Anti-dumping duties are regularly imposed in the form of regulations, although they do in fact have individual addressees, as was recognised in Case C-358/89 *Extramet Industrie SA* v. *Council* [1991] ECR I-2501. Such so-called disguised decisions are commonly challenged before the ECJ, and now also before the CFI.

The ECJ's restrictive stance on the *locus standi* of individuals in challenges of regulations has remained controversial even to the point that the two Community courts have split in their views, and one advocate-general has sharply criticised the existing case law in Case C-50/00P *Unión de Pequeños Agricultores* v. *Council* [2002] ECR I-6677. In Case T-177/01 *Jégo-Quéré* v. *Commission* [2002] ECR II-2365, the CFI adopted a more liberal approach which, on appeal, was promptly overruled by the ECJ in Case C-263/02P *Commission* v. *Jégo-Quéré* [2004] ECR I-3425. Suffice it to note that the Draft Constitution Treaty (→ *1.9*) as well as the Lisbon Reform Treaty (→ *1.10*) would have liberalised the standing rules by no longer requiring 'individual' but only 'direct' concern in the case of regulatory acts.

5.7 What is a 'plea of illegality'?

A plea of illegality is not a distinctive form of action. Instead, Article 241 TEC allows an indirect challenge to regulations even after the two-month time-limit for annulment actions has expired. In Cases 31 and 33/62 *Milchwerke Heinz Wohrmann & Sohn and Alfons Lütticke GmbH* v. *Commission* [1962] ECR 501, the ECJ stated that Article 241 TEC cannot be used before national courts, but only before the ECJ itself. It further clarified that Article 241 TEC does not permit a direct challenge under Article 230 TEC once the time-limit has expired because 'the sole object of Article 184 [now Article 241 TEC] is thus to protect an interested party against the application of an illegal regulation, without thereby in any way calling in issue the regulation itself which can no longer be challenged because of the expiry of the time limit laid down in Article 173 [now Article 230 TEC].'

Typically, a plea of illegality may be used to assert the illegality of a regulation on which a challenged decision is based as in Case 92/78 *Simmenthal SpA* v. *Commission* [1979] ECR 777, where the ECJ held that Article 241 TEC 'enables the applicant to challenge indirectly during the proceedings, with a view to obtaining the annulment of the contested decisions, the validity of the measures laid down by Regulation which form the legal basis of the latter.'

According to Case 66/80, *International Chemical Corporation* v. *Amministrazione delle Finanze dello Stato* [1981] ECR 1191, a successful plea of illegality in the course of a preliminary reference does **not** lead to **formal annulment** but constitutes 'sufficient reason for any other national court to regard that act as void'.

? 5.8 For what reasons may the ECJ invalidate Community acts?

Article 230 TEC specifies four **grounds of invalidity,** which are also valid for purposes of preliminary rulings according to Article 234 ($\rightarrow$ *5.14*) and under a plea of illegality pursuant to Article 241 TEC ($\rightarrow$ *5.7*):

(1) **lack of competence;**
(2) **infringement** of an **essential procedural safeguard;**
(3) **infringement** of the **Treaty** or any **rule of law relating to its application;** and
(4) **misuse of powers.**

Lack of competence and **Treaty infringements** are relatively straightforward grounds for annulment. **Lack of competence** is usually invoked when it is alleged that EU institutions have violated the principle of **enumerated powers** ($\rightarrow$ *3.1, 5.4*) enshrined in Article 7(1) TEC by exceeding the powers transferred to them. Lawyers refer to such acts that are 'beyond the powers' of an organ as '*ultra vires*' acts. Any **inconsistency of Community legislation** with the **provisions of the TEC** may be raised in an annulment action alleging **infringement** of the **Treaty.** The somewhat more mysterious formulation of infringements of 'any rule of law relating to [the TEC's] application' has been broadly interpreted by the ECJ to cover not only implementing law, but also **international agreements** ($\rightarrow$ *11.3*) as well as

fundamental rights (→ *6.7*), which are considered to be general principles of Community law.

The annulment ground of **misuse of powers**, stemming from the French administrative law concept of 'detournément de pouvoir', has only rarely been successfully invoked before the Community courts. Basically, it occurs when Community institutions **use** their **powers** to **obtain an objective** for which the powers were **not intended**. The infringement of an essential procedural safeguard, however, has been made more precise in a considerable body of ECJ case law.

? 5.9 Give examples of infringements of essential procedural safeguards

For example, in Case 138/79 *Roquettes Frères SA* v. *Council* [1980] ECR 3333, the Court used its power of **judicial review** to strengthen considerably the constitutional position of the European Parliament in the **law-making process**. It annulled a Council regulation which had been adopted without proper regard to the **consultation** procedure provided for under the pertinent Treaty provision (→ *3.5*). In the Court's view 'due consultation of the Parliament in the cases provided for by the Treaty therefore constitutes an essential formality disregard of which means that the measure concerned is void'.

In the so-called *Branntwein* (German for *Brandy*) Case, Case 24/62 *Germany* v. *Commission* [1963] ECR 63, the Court found a breach of the **duty to provide reasons** (→ *3.2*). In its view, a Commission decision approving a lower rate of import of wine failed to state reasons as required by Article 253 TEC by merely saying that 'on the basis of existing information' wine production in the Community was amply sufficient. In a later case, Case C-76/01P *Eurocoton and others* v. *Council* [2003] ECR I-10091, the ECJ clarified that:

the statement of reasons required by Article [253 TEC]
must be appropriate to the act at issue and must disclose
in a clear and unequivocal fashion the reasoning followed
by the institution which adopted the measure in question
in such way as to enable the persons concerned to
ascertain the reasons for the measure and to enable the
competent Community Court to exercise its power of
review.

In Case 17/74 *Transocean Marine Paint* v. *Commission* [1974]
ECR 1063, it was the requirement to provide a hearing (→ *6.4*)
which was violated in the eyes of the ECJ. The Court demanded
that 'a person whose interests are perceptibly affected by a decision taken by a public authority must be given the opportunity
to make his point of view known'. Thus, a Commission decision
granting a renewal of competition law exemptions according to
Article 81(3) TEC (→ *9.12*) under new conditions upon which
the addressee could not comment was invalidated. The right to
a fair hearing was equally recognised in anti-dumping procedures (→ *11.2*) in Case C-49/88 *Al-Jubail* v. *Council* [1991] ECR
I-3187, and in customs law (→ *11.2*) in Case C-269 *Technische
Universität München* v. *Hauptzollamt München-Mitte* [1991]
ECR I-5469.

5.10 Do the judgments and rulings of the ECJ have retroactive effect?

In principle, judgments and rulings of the ECJ have retroac-
tive effect because they are merely declaratory statements of
what has always been the correct interpretation of the law even
before formal annulment. However, Article 231(2) TEC allows
the Court to qualify the extent of the nullity.

In case of serious financial implications, the Court has also
held that its preliminary rulings (→ *5.14–19*) may have only

prospective effect. In the follow-up to the famous 'equal pay' case of *Defrenne*, Case 43/75 *Defrenne* v. *Sabena (Defrenne II)* [1976] ECR 455 ($\rightarrow$ *4.5, 10.17*), the ECJ ruled that for 'important considerations of legal certainty' the 'direct effect of Article 119 cannot be relied on in order to support claims concerning pay periods prior to the date of this judgment'. The Court's interpretation of Article 119 (now Article 141) TEC ($\rightarrow$ *10.17*) as being directly applicable Community law from the end of the transitional period could have driven many employers into bankruptcy.

Independent of any such qualification by the Court, Article 233(1) TEC provides that any Community institution 'whose act has been declared void . . . shall be required to take the necessary measures to comply with the judgment of the Court'.

? 5.11 What are the stages leading to an Article 226 TEC procedure?

The peculiar sequencing of an enforcement action against Member States is the result of the multiple purposes it pursues. It is intended to give the Commission considerable supervisory power ($\rightarrow$ *2.13*), to offer individuals indirect access for their complaints (although the Commission is under no duty to act upon private complaints) and to provide room for diplomatic settlement. Infringement proceedings involve four distinct stages:

(1) in the pre-contentious stage, the Commission and the Member State concerned merely engage in negotiations which may informally resolve the matter;

(2) if this is not the case, the 'letter from Brussels' will formally notify the Member State of the specific infringement allegations. This Commission 'letter of notice' requires a reasonable time (usually two months) for a reply;

(3) if negotiations are still unsuccessful, the administrative stage will move on to the judicial stage. The Commission will issue a **'reasoned opinion'** (Article 226 TEC), which clearly spells out the grounds for the alleged infringement and calls for remedial action within a specified time period; and

(4) if the Member State does not comply with the Commission's opinion, the latter may **institute proceedings** before the ECJ.

5.12 What is the legal effect of an Article 226 TEC ruling?

The result of a successful infringement action is a **declaratory judgment**. However, according to Article 228(1) TEC, Member States are required to take the **necessary measures** to **comply** with the judgment of the Court. Next to remedial steps, such as abolition of national law found in violation of EC law, national authorities are no longer permitted to apply domestic rules violating EC law as a result of **supremacy** (→ *4.11, 4.12*).

In addition, the Maastricht Treaty Amendment (→ *1.8*) introduced in Article 228(2) TEC the possibility of awarding a 'lump sum or penalty payment' in cases of **non-compliance** by Member States. In Case C-387/97 *Commission* v. *Greece* [2000] ECR I-5047, the first case decided under the new provision, the Court basically accepted the Commission's guidelines and awarded penalty payments of €20,000 per day of non-compliance with the initial judgment. It accepted that the 'basic criteria which must be taken into account in order to ensure that penalty payments have coercive force . . . are, in principle, the **duration** of the infringement, its degree of **seriousness** and the **ability** of the Member State **to pay**'. Recently, in Case C-304/02 *Commission* v. *France* [2005] ECR I-6263, the ECJ imposed both a lump sum and a penalty payment arguing, in an exemplary fashion of **teleological** reasoning, that 'in the light of the objective pursued by Article 228 EC, the conjunction "or" in Article 228(2) EC must be understood as being used in a cumulative sense.'

? 5.13 Can the violation of Community law by a Member State be easily justified?

Member States have been rather ingenious in developing **defences** of their EC law infringements. The ECJ, however, has not been very receptive to the arguments brought forward in this context.

Noting that Member States are free to challenge Community acts under the **annulment procedure** (→ *5.5–10*) the Court held in Case 226/87 *Commission* v. *Greece* [1988] ECR 3611, that 'a Member State cannot therefore plead the unlawfulness of a decision addressed to it as a defence in an action for a declaration that it has failed to fulfil its obligations arising out of its failure to implement that decision'. Thus, **Member States** are under a **duty to comply** with EC law **until annulled** by the ECJ. The only exceptions may be found in particularly serious and manifest defects of Community measures that might qualify as non-existent acts that need not be followed.

In Case 7/61 *Commission* v. *Italy* [1964] ECR 635, the ECJ held that an **emergency procedure** provided for in the TEC, which required express Commission authorisation for an import ban on pork, **excluded** any **unilateral measures** by Member States.

In Joined Cases 90 and 91/63 *Commission* v. *Luxembourg and Belgium* [1964] ECR 1217, the Court held that the '*tu quoque*' excuse under international law, allowing suspension or withdrawal of treaty performance as a consequence of another party's failure to perform, 'cannot be recognised under Community law'. In the Court's view, even where a Community institution failed to carry out its obligations, 'the basic concept of the Treaty requires that Member States shall not fail to carry out their obligations and shall not take the law into their own hands'. Similarly, in Case C-146/89 *Commission* v. *United Kingdom* [1991] ECR 3533, the Court has consistently held that 'under the legal order established by the Treaty, the implementation of Community law by Member States cannot be made subject to a condition of reciprocity'.

It is clear from the ECJ's case law that a Member State may not plead constitutional, administrative or institutional difficulties in complying with EC law. In Case 77/69 *Commission* v. *Belgium* [1970] ECR 237, the Court refused to regard the dissolution of a national parliament as *force majeure* preventing the adoption of implementing legislation. It equally rejected the Belgian separation of powers argument stating unequivocally that 'liability of a Member State . . . arises whatever the agency of the State whose action or inaction is the cause of the failure to fulfil its obligations, even in the case of a constitutionally independent institution'. In another case against Belgium, Case 301/81 *Commission* v. *Belgium* [1983] ECR 467, the ECJ went so far as to assert that 'only . . . an objective finding of a failure' to implement a directive on credit institutions was relevant for the infringement action. In Case C-129/00 *Commission* v. *Italy* [2003] ECR I-14637 the ECJ held that even the judgments of a Member State's highest court may entail that Member's responsibility.

5.14 What is a preliminary reference?

According to Article 234 TEC, the ECJ:

> shall have jurisdiction to give preliminary rulings concerning:

(a) the interpretation of the Treaty;
(b) the validity and interpretation of acts of the
institutions of the Community and of the ECB;
(c) the interpretation of the statutes of bodies established
by an act of the Council, where those statutes so
provide.

Where such a question is raised before any court or
tribunal of a Member State, that court or tribunal may, if
it considers that a decision on the question is necessary
to enable it to give judgment, request the Court of Justice
to give a ruling thereon.

The Nice Treaty (→ *1.8*) provides for the possibility of also
submitting certain preliminary references to the CFI (→ *5.3*),
which might further help the ECJ to reduce its case-load in the
future.

In practice, requests for the interpretation of Community
acts, that is, regulations, directives, decisions, recommendations with legal effects and international agreements (→ *ch. 3*),
are the most frequent uses of the preliminary reference procedure made by national courts.

? 5.15 May national courts invalidate secondary EC law?

In Case 314/85 *Firma Foto Frost* v. *Hauptzollamt Lübeck-Ost*
[1987] ECR 4199, the Court affirmed that 'requests for preliminary rulings, like actions for annulment, constitute means
for reviewing the legality of acts of the Community institutions'. When a German court asked whether it could declare
a Commission decision in the field of external trade invalid,
the ECJ rejected this idea insisting on its own exclusive right of
invalidating Community law. The Court reasoned that it was
one of the main purposes of Article 234 TEC:

to ensure that Community law is applied uniformly by national law. That requirement of uniformity is particularly imperative when the validity of a Community act is in question. Divergences between courts in the Member States as to the validity of Community acts would be liable to place in jeopardy the very unity of the Community legal order and detract from the fundamental requirements of legal certainty.

5.16 What is a 'tribunal' for the purposes of Article 234 TEC and when is it obliged to ask for a preliminary ruling?

According to Case 246/80 *Broekmeulen* v. *Huisarts Registratie Commissie* [1981] ECR 2311, the Dutch Appeals Committee for General Medicine was recognised as a 'tribunal' because it operated with the **consent** and **cooperation** of **public authorities**, used **adversarial procedures** and delivered **final decisions**. In addition to these characteristics, general establishment by law, permanency, compulsory jurisdiction, *inter partes* procedure, independence and applying rules of law, are seen as criteria to be evaluated when determining whether a decision-making body qualifies as a 'court or tribunal' enabled to ask for a preliminary ruling. The **status** (public authority) and **function** (independent judicial tasks) seem to be the guiding principles for the ECJ. After *Broekmeulen* other professional, including disciplinary, bodies, tax and immigration adjudicators, as well as review bodies for public contracts have been held to qualify as 'tribunals' in the sense of Article 234 TEC. Though 'tribunal' is a wide term, it does **not** include **arbitral tribunals**. In Case 102/81 *Nordsee Deutsche Hochseefischerei* [1982] ECR 1095, the ECJ qualified commercial arbitration as a form of private and not state dispute settlement.

According to Article 234(2) TEC 'any court or tribunal of a Member State' may request a preliminary ruling. However, pursuant to Article 234(3) TEC, tribunals 'against whose decision there is no judicial remedy under national law' **have to** make a **request** for a preliminary ruling. Since the ECJ favours the **'concrete'** over the 'abstract' theory, this is not necessarily the highest court but the court having the **final say** in the **special case**, as was confirmed in Case C-99/00 *Lyckeskog* [2002] ECR I-4839.

However, the obligation to make a preliminary reference is in practice limited by the so-called *'acte clair'* doctrine, which provides a certain amount of discretion to national courts as to whether they consider a ruling 'necessary' for their ensuing judgment (→ *5.19*).

5.17 Are there preliminary ruling procedures other than Article 234 TEC?

The Amsterdam Treaty Amendments (→ *1.8*) entailed two further **preliminary ruling procedures**: first, Article 68(1) TEC, which is part of the new Title IV concerning visas, asylum and immigration – matters of the former third pillar (**Justice and Home Affairs**) that were moved into the first (**Community**) pillar by the Amsterdam Treaty (→ *2.1*) – provides that preliminary rulings may be sought in this area by tribunals 'against whose decision there is no judicial remedy under national law'.

Second, Article 35(1) TEU, in the old 'Justice and Home Affairs' pillar, and after Amsterdam now 'Police and Judicial Co-operation in Criminal Matters' (→ *2.1*), opens up the possibility of preliminary rulings on the interpretation and validity of certain PJCC measures. This requires, however, a specific **'opt in'**, a declaration of acceptance by Member States.

? 5.18 Does the ECJ decide on all requests for preliminary rulings?

The ECJ does not have to rule on all requests. Rather, it has consistently insisted on its discretion to reserve the preliminary ruling procedure to 'genuine disputes'.

Case 104/79 *Foglia* v. *Novello* [1980] ECR 745, is one of the first cases where the ECJ limited access to the sometimes overly successful Article 234 TEC procedure. Foglia sold wine to Novello stipulating that Novello should not pay for any taxes charged in violation of EC law. Although Foglia had a similar clause in his carriage contract with his general transporter, he reimbursed the transporter for French taxes, which were believed to be contrary to EC law, and passed these charges on to Novello in his invoice. When Novello refused to pay, Foglia sued in Italian courts. The ECJ declared a request for a preliminary ruling **inadmissible** because Article 234 TEC required a 'genuine dispute' and not a **hypothetical case.**

When the Italian court made a second request in Case 244/80 *Foglia* v. *Novello (No. 2)* [1981] ECR 3045, speculating on the consistency of the ECJ's first ruling under the principle that it was for the national courts to assess the necessity for a reference, the Court reaffirmed its earlier decision stressing that it would **not** render 'advisory opinions'.

The *Foglia* cases have been very controversial since they may be interpreted as giving the Court a wide-ranging discretion to pick and choose those cases it wishes to hear. Still, the Court has reaffirmed in Case C-341/01 *Plato Plastik* v. *Caropack* [2004] ECR I-4883, that it:

> has no jurisdiction to give a preliminary ruling on a
> question submitted by a national court where it is quite
> obvious that the interpretation or assessment of the
> validity of a Community rule sought by that court bears

no relation to the facts or purpose of the main action, where the problem is hypothetical or where the Court does not have before it the factual or legal material necessary to enable it to give a useful answer to the questions submitted to it.

5.19 When is a ruling on a preliminary question 'necessary' to enable a national court to give judgment?

Next to the *Foglia* requirement of a 'genuine dispute' ($\rightarrow$ *5.18*), the only other effective safety valve ensuring that the ECJ may limit the case-load of references brought to it is the acceptance of the **acte clair** doctrine ($\rightarrow$ *5.16*), originally devised by national courts which were hesitant to make references.

In *Bulmer* v. *Bollinger* [1974] 2 WLR 202, Lord Denning of the English Court of Appeal laid down the following guidelines as to whether a decision is 'necessary': (a) the point must be **conclusive**; (b) **previous rulings** are relevant and, as a rule, they should be followed by national courts, and only if they think that a previous ruling may have been wrong should they re-submit the point to the ECJ; and (c) if a point is 'reasonably clear and free from doubt' it constitutes an '*acte clair*' and 'there is no need to interpret the Treaty but only to apply it'.

The *acte clair* doctrine was accepted by the ECJ in Case 283/81 *CILFIT* v. *Ministero della Sanita* [1982] ECR 3415, where the Court accepted that the 'correct application of Community law may be so obvious as to leave no scope for any reasonable doubt'. The Court cautioned, however, that only if the matter was 'equally obvious to the courts of other Member States' and to the ECJ itself, may a national court 'refrain from submitting a question to the Court of Justice'.

6 Protecting fundamental rights within the Community

The **initial Community treaties** establishing the ECSC, the EEC and EURATOM did **not** contain **any fundamental rights** provisions at all. The 1953 Draft Treaty embodying the Statute of a European Political Community envisaged human rights protection as a major task and proposed to incorporate the **European Convention on Human Rights** (ECHR), a treaty concluded by many European states in 1950 under the auspices of the **Council of Europe** and enforced by the **European Court of Human Rights** (ECtHR) in Strasbourg. After the plans for a European Defence Community were buried by the French National Assembly in 1954, this idea also became **obsolete**. With the resurgence of the 'functionalist approach', culminating in the 1957 Rome Treaties, the view prevailed that the economic integration now pursued did **not warrant** the inclusion of **human rights** guarantees.

With the growth of Community activities, however, the likelihood of **infringement** of fundamental rights also **increased**. Clearly, the extension of Community law into many fields beyond the core aspects of the four freedoms was not a wholly unintended 'spill-over effect' of economic integration. This tendency was reinforced by the specific development of EC law, in particular of **direct effect** and **supremacy** in such landmark cases as *Van Gend en Loos* and *Costa* v. *ENEL*. Both direct effect and supremacy increase the probability that it is EC law itself and not any national implementation of Community obligations that may infringe human rights.

Again, it was the **ECJ** which played a crucial role in **developing** a **fundamental rights protection** within the Community. The Court found that fundamental rights constituted an integral part of the **general principles of law** which were binding upon the Community, and it identified a number of specific basic rights through a comparative exercise looking at the **constitutions** of the Member States and **drawing inspiration** from the **ECHR**. It was only after the Maastricht Treaty amendments that this approach was codified and integrated into the text of the TEU. However, the incorporation of a full **'bill of rights'**, containing specific fundamental rights, remains a controversial task.

This chapter will explain the gradual development of the ECJ's **jurisprudence** on the protection of fundamental rights against potential infringements by acts of the Community institutions.

6.1 What were the initial responses of the ECJ to calls for a human rights protection?

The **initial reaction** of the **ECJ** to human rights arguments was not very promising. In Case 1/58 *Stork* v. *High Authority* [1959] ECR 17, Joined Cases 36, 37, 38 and 40/59 *Geitling* v. *High Authority* [1960] ECR 423, and Case 40/64 *Sgarlata* v. *High Authority* [1965] ECR 215, the Court denied the possibility of examining alleged infringements of national constitutional law by the adoption of Community acts. It also **denied** the existence of any **general principles** in Community law **protecting** vested **rights**, as well as the possibility that fundamental principles common to the legal systems of all the Member States could override an express Treaty provision.

Only pressure by courts in some Member States, particularly the Italian and German constitutional courts (→ *6.10–12*), as a reaction to the ECJ's **supremacy** doctrine (→ *4.10, 4.11*) which would encroach upon domestic human rights protection, ultimately led to a change in the ECJ's jurisprudence.

6.2 What was the role of the ECJ in developing fundamental rights protection?

In the absence of a clear Treaty mandate to scrutinise the compliance of the institutions of the Community in the area of fundamental rights, the ECJ used its powers of judicial review ($\rightarrow$ 5.8) of Community acts in order to check whether they conformed with legal principles which it gradually interpreted in an ever more expansive way.

One of the first cases reflecting such a new approach was Case 29/69 *Stauder* v. *Stadt Ulm* [1969] ECR 419. In order to reduce the Community's butter surplus a Commission decision authorised Member States to make butter available to social assistance recipients at lower cost. Persons claiming the benefit had to present certain coupons to retailers. The German text of the decision provided for the identification of the recipient. Stauder, a war victim, considered the identification requirement to be contrary to his constitutionally guaranteed right to privacy. A German administrative court asked the ECJ for a preliminary ruling on this matter. In *Stauder*, the ECJ for the first time acknowledged the relevance of fundamental rights for the Community. The Court held that 'the provision in question must be interpreted as not requiring – although it does not prohibit – the identification of beneficiaries by name'; it thus 'contains nothing capable of prejudicing the fundamental human rights enshrined in the general principles of Community law and protected by the Court'.

In Case 4/73 *Nold* v. *Commission* [1974] ECR 491, the ECJ broadened the sources of inspiration when it came to ascertaining specific fundamental rights as forming general principles of law. In addition to the 'constitutional traditions common to the Member States', the Court also found that 'international **treaties** for the **protection of human rights** on which the Member States have collaborated or of which they are signatories, can supply guidelines which should be followed within the framework of Community law'. In the particular case, a new Community decision required that the German national coal producer, Ruhrkohle, would sell only to large wholesalers on two-year contracts. Nold, a small wholesaler, who under the previous system purchased directly from Ruhrkohle, considered this to be a violation of his right to property and his freedom to pursue economic activities. Nold sued the Commission directly under Article 230(4) TEC (→ *5.6*). Though the Court reaffirmed its position that 'fundamental rights form an integral part of the general principles of law, the observance of which it ensures', it found no violation of such rights in this particular case. It justified this by holding that rights of ownership do not protect 'mere commercial opportunities'.

Similarly, in Case 44/79 *Hauer* v. *Land Rheinland-Pfalz* [1979] ECR 3727, the ECJ recognised the right to own property as one of the general principles of Community law to be respected by Community legislation. However, after a careful analysis of various national constitutional provisions restricting the use of real property for various public interests, it found that a Council regulation prohibiting the planting of vines in certain areas did not violate this right.

? 6.3 Does the ECJ recognise the same rights as the European Court of Human Rights?

In practice, the ECJ is not only guided by international human rights instruments like the ECHR, but also by the specific interpretation given to its articles by the ECtHR. Nevertheless, sometimes the **interpretation** of ECHR rights adopted by the **ECJ** may **differ** from that of the **ECtHR** in Strasbourg.

This happened with regard to the **right to privacy**, which the ECJ interpreted rather restrictively. In Case 136/79 *National Panasonic* v. *Commission* [1980] ECR 2033, the Court upheld the legality of Commission investigations on commercial premises. Similarly in Joined Cases 97–99/87 *Dow Chemical Ibérica and others* v. *Commission* [1989] ECR 3165, the ECJ held that Article 8 ECHR, according to which 'everyone has the right to respect for his private and family life, his home and his correspondence' was **limited to private dwellings** of private persons, and 'may not therefore be extended to business premises'.

This contrasts with the broader interpretation given to Article 8 ECHR by the ECtHR in cases like *Niemetz* v. *Germany* (1993) 16 EHRR 97, where the court in Strasbourg held that the right to privacy also **encompassed business premises** where this was necessary to protect the individual against arbitrary interference by public authorities.

6.4 Which other human rights have been accepted in the jurisprudence of the ECJ?

Over the years the ECJ and the CFI have recognised a considerable number of fundamental rights, not only of an economic nature, which include:

(1) **freedom** to practice one's **religion**: Case 130/75 *Prais* v. *Council* [1976] ECR 1589;

(2) **respect** for **private life**: Case 165/82 *Commission* v. *United Kingdom* [1976] ECR;

(3) **protection** of **personal data**: Joined Cases C-456/00, C-138/01 and C-139/01 *Rechnungshof* v. *Österreichischer Rundfunk* [2003] ECR I-4919;

(4) **freedom of expression**: Case 100/88 *Oyowe and Traore* v. *Commission* [1989] ECR 4285, Case 34/79 *R.* v. *Henn and Darby* [1979] ECR 3975, Case C-274/99P *Connolly* v. *Commission* [2001] ECR I-1611;

(5) the **right** to form **trade unions**: Case 175/73 *Union Syndicale* v. *Council* [1974] ECR 917;

(6) the **right** to an effective **judicial remedy**: Case 222/84 *Johnston* v. *RUC* [1986] ECR 1651;

(7) the **right to be heard**: Case 17/74 *Transocean Marine Paint* v. *Commission* [1974] ECR 1063 (→ *5.9*);

(8) the right against **self-incrimination**: Case 374/87 *Orkem* v. *Commission* [1989] ECR 3283;

(9) the right to freely **pursue trade** and professional activities: Case 230/78 *SpA Eridania Zuccherifici nazionali and others* v. *Minister of Agriculture and Forestry* [1979] ECR 2749; and

(10) **equality** (equal pay): Case 43/75 *Defrenne* v. *Sabena* [1976] ECR 455 (→ *4.5, 5.10, 10.17*).

? 6.5 Which general principles of law has the ECJ identified?

In addition to the fundamental rights identified by the ECJ as general principles of Community law, which largely correspond to human rights guarantees found in many national constitutions as well as in international agreements, the Court has also elaborated on a number of **general principles** which are more akin to **principles of administrative law**, such as proportionality, equal treatment, legal certainty and legitimate expectations.

In Case 122/78 *Buitoni SA* v. *Fonds d'Orientation et de Régularisation des Marchés Agricoles* [1979] ECR 677, the ECJ scrutinised a Commission regulation providing for the forfeiture of security deposits for the importation of agricultural goods if import formalities had not been completed in time. Here the Court found, however, that, particularly when the imports themselves were made timely, the system was 'excessively severe in relation to the objectives of administrative efficiency' and, thus, not in line with the requirements of **proportionality** (→ *6.9*).

In the so-called *Skimmed Milk* Case, Case 114/76 *Bela-Mühle Josef Bergmann KG* v. *Grows-Farm GmbH & Co. KG* [1977] ECR 1211, the Court combined **proportionality** and **equal treatment** as major grounds for invalidating a Community act in the field of agriculture. The challenged regulation aimed at the reduction of a milk surplus in the Community by requiring animal feed producers to use skimmed milk as a protein ingredient instead of cheaper alternatives. *Bela-Mühle* refused to pay its supplier the resulting price increase, maintaining that the regulation was invalid. The ECJ found an imposition of a financial burden not only on milk producers, but also on producers in other agricultural sectors in the form of the compulsory purchase and the price-fixing at a threefold level. It held that the 'obligation to purchase at such a disproportionate price constituted a discriminatory distribution of the burden of costs between the various agricultural sectors'.

The related principles of **legal certainty** and **legitimate expectations** have also figured prominently in the ECJ's jurisprudence. In Case 98/78 *Firma A. Racke* v. *Hauptzollamt Mainz* [1979] ECR 69, the Court found that 'in general the principle of legal certainty precludes a Community measure from taking effect from a point in time before its publication . . .', thus, affirming also the principle of non-retroactivity.

The first *Mulder* Case (→ *10.5*), Case 120/86 *Mulder* v. *Minister van Landbouw en Visserij* [1988] ECR 2321, illustrates how the disappointment of **legitimate expectations** may lead to the annulment of a Community act. The ECJ invalidated a 1984 Council regulation under which a Dutch farmer had agreed not to market milk for a five-year period, and was refused permission to resume production after that period because quotas were issued on the basis of production levels of the previous years. The Court considered this to be a violation of the producer's legitimate expectations, because 'where such a producer, as in the present case, has been encouraged by a Community measure to suspend marketing for a limited period in the general interest and against payment of a premium he may legitimately expect not to be subject, upon the expiry of his undertaking, to restrictions which specifically affect him precisely because he availed himself of the possibilities offered by the Community provisions'.

6.6 Where does the Court find fundamental rights in Community law?

Although the Treaty does not contain any fundamental rights provisions comparable to domestic constitutional rights, there is an 'analogous guarantee inherent in Community law'. In Case 11/70 *Internationale Handelsgesellschaft* v. *Einfuhr- und Vorratsstelle für Getreide und Futtermittel* [1970] ECR 1125 the ECJ held that:

> respect for fundamental rights forms an integral part of the general principles of law protected by the Court of Justice. The protection of such rights, whilst inspired by the constitutional traditions common to the Member States, must be ensured within the framework of the structure and objectives of the Community.

6.7 How does the Court protect fundamental rights as a matter of procedure?

Since the TEC provisions on the jurisdiction of the ECJ do not provide for a fundamental rights complaint, the Court had to find a way to extend its powers over such cases. As a result of the principle of enumerated powers, which binds all European institutions (→3.1, 5.8), the ECJ can act only within the scope of powers transferred to it. Human rights scrutiny is not expressly mentioned in the jurisdictional provisions of the Treaty. The court does, however, interpret its express **mandate** broadly and regards human rights protection as forming part of its general task under Article 220 TEC, namely 'to **ensure** that in the interpretation and application of this Treaty **the law is observed**'.

More specifically, it considers fundamental rights violations of Community acts as constituting grounds for **annulment** under Article 230(2) TEC, being an 'infringement of this Treaty or of any rule of law relating to its application' (→ 5.8). The general principles of Community law, of which fundamental rights form an integral part, are regarded as rules of law relating to the Treaty's application. In a similar vein, the ECJ has shown its willingness to test the validity of Community acts in preliminary references (→ 5.14).

? 6.8 Is the EU bound to respect the ECHR?

In a technical sense, the Community is not formally bound by the ECHR. **Only** its **Member States** are **Contracting Parties** of the Convention. In the early 1990s the Commission proposed that the Community should formally accede to the ECHR. But in 1996 the ECJ delivered its Advisory Opinion 2/94 on the *Accession of the Community to the European Convention on Human Rights* [1996] ECR I-1759, according to which an accession was not possible on the basis of then existing Community law. Although the Court couched its ruling in terms of lack of Community competence (→ 3.1), many observers felt that the underlying reason may have been the court's reluctance to accept a superior court as final arbiter in fundamental rights matters. Article I-7(2) of the **Draft Constitution Treaty** would have expressly enabled the EU to **accede** to the ECHR.

As far as the substance is concerned, however, the Court's approach towards fundamental rights protection was already endorsed by a 1977 **Joint Declaration** of the Parliament, the Council and the Commission, [1977] OJ C103/1, in which the institutions formally committed themselves to ensuring **respect** for **fundamental rights** in the **exercise of their powers**. It equally found its expression in the preamble to the SEA which spoke of the willingness 'to promote democracy on the basis of the fundamental rights recognized in the constitutions and laws of the Member States, in the Convention for the Protection of Human Rights and Fundamental Freedoms and the European Social Charter, notably freedom, equality and social justice'.

Today, the ECJ's **jurisprudence** is encapsulated or, as lawyers would say, **codified** in Article 6(2) TEU which provides as follows:

> The Union shall respect fundamental rights, as **guaranteed** by the **European Convention for the Protection of Human Rights and Fundamental Freedoms** signed in Rome on 4 November 1950 and as they **result** from the **constitutional traditions** common to the Member States, as **general principles of Community law**.

6.9 Why is the Internationale Handelsgesellschaft Case so important?

In Case 11/70 *Internationale Handelsgesellschaft* v. *Einfuhr- und Vorratsstelle für Getreide und Futtermittel* [1970] ECR 1125, the ECJ held that the Community's forfeiture scheme of an export licensing system did not violate general principles of law. It was a rather technical case; however, it is of particular importance for the development of fundamental rights protection in the EC as a prelude to the German *Solange I* Case discussed below (→ *6.10*).

The facts of the case are as follows: under a 1967 Council regulation, export licences for certain agricultural products were conditional upon prior payment of a deposit, which was to be forfeited if the export was not made. This forfeiture provision was challenged before a German administrative court, which thought that the system violated principles of the German Basic Law (that is, the German Constitution), *inter alia*, the freedom of disposition and proportionality, and that EC law must yield before these principles. Still, the German court referred the question to the ECJ.

The ECJ affirmed the primacy of EC law even vis-à-vis national constitutional law (→ *4.10*). It did, however, hold that 'analogous guarantees inherent in Community law' must be respected. Nevertheless, according to the ECJ, the forfeiture deposit system was 'necessary and appropriate to enable the competent authorities to determine in the most effective manner their interventions on the market of cereals'. In doing so it formulated important principles of Community proportionality (→ *6.5*): that is, Community action must be relevant and necessary to the attainment of a Community objective, and the aggregate burden upon affected persons must be no greater than that which is needed for the attainment of that objective.

6.10 What was the Solange I Case?

Both *Solange* (literally: 'as long as') decisions were rendered by the German Federal Constitutional Court. *Solange I*, as *Internationale Handelsgesellschaft* v. *Einfuhr- und Vorratsstelle für Getreide und Futtermittel* [1974] 2 CMLR 540, is usually referred to, relates to the *Internationale Handelsgesellschaft* Case of the ECJ (→ *6.9*). After the ECJ's decision the applicant referred to the German Constitutional Court, asking basically the same question and contending that the scheme contravened fundamental human rights provisions of the **German Constitution**, that is, the Bonn Basic Law.

The Constitutional Court held that Article 24 of the Basic Law ('The Federation may by legislation transfer sovereign powers to intergovernmental institutions') was **inherently limiting** ('Integrationsschranke'), insofar as it nullified any primary or secondary Community law which would 'destroy the identity of the valid constitution of the Federal Republic of Germany'. Since '**fundamental rights** [were] an **inalienable** essential **feature** of the valid **Constitution** of the Federal Republic of Germany' the limitation of Article 24 of the Basic Law applied. As a result, Community law not complying with German fundamental rights guarantees could not be applied by German authorities. '**As long as**' the **EC** had **no adequate human rights** catalogue, the Constitutional Court would have **jurisdiction** to rule on the compatibility with the Basic Law and, thus, the applicability in Germany of a Community law norm. On the merits, however, it was held that the contested system did not violate German human rights guarantees.

6.11 Why was there a Solange II Case?

Wünsche Handelsgesellschaft [1987] 3 CMLR 225, the so-called *Solange II* decision of the German Federal Constitutional Court, was rendered in 1986. A German importer, having been denied licences under a Community system, claimed a violation of his right to a fair hearing. The Constitutional

Court essentially affirmed its previous jurisprudence concerning Article 24 of the Basic Law. It reaffirmed that there were inherent limitations to the transfer of sovereign powers, but it altered its view on the human rights guarantees provided by the Community. It held that they were 'essentially comparable' or 'substantially similar' to those under the German Constitution. The German Court thereby recognised that in the time between the two *Solange* decisions the ECJ had developed an established case law protecting fundamental rights.

Thus, the Court concluded that 'as long as' the EC 'generally ensured an effective protection of fundamental rights as against the sovereign powers of the Communities' that were 'substantially similar' to that of the German Constitution – safeguarding the essential content of fundamental rights – the Federal Constitutional Court 'will no longer exercise its jurisdiction' to decide upon the applicability of secondary EC law as the basis for acts of German organs within Germany. As a result the complaint was inadmissible.

? 6.12 Were other national courts also reluctant to accept full supremacy of EC law?

The German Constitutional Court was not alone in its scepticism towards an unbound supremacy of EC law. In a ruling similar to the *Solange I* decision, the Italian Constitutional Court held in *Frontini* v. *Ministero delle Finanze* [1974] 2 CMLR 372, that:

> by Article 11 of the Constitution limitations of sovereignty are allowed solely for the purpose of the ends indicated therein, and it should therefore be excluded that such limitations of sovereignty, concretely laid out in the Rome Treaty, signed by countries whose systems are based on the principle of the rule of law and guarantee the essential liberties of citizens, can nevertheless give

the organs of the EEC an unacceptable power to violate
the fundamental principles of our constitutional order
or the inalienable rights of man. And it is obvious that if
ever Article [249 TEC] had to be given such an aberrant
interpretation, in such a case the guarantee would always
be assured that this Court would control the continuing
compatibility of the Treaty with the above mentioned
fundamental principles.

? 6.13 Discuss the importance of the Wachauf and subsequent cases addressing the relationship between Community and Member State measures

The fundamental rights jurisprudence of the ECJ was primarily
concerned with challenges directed against Community acts.
Since Community law is often implemented by national authorities, sooner or later the question had to arise as to whether and
to what extent **Member States** are bound to **respect fundamental rights** when **implementing** and applying Community law.

Case 5/88 *Wachauf* v. *Germany* [1989] ECR 2609 is the leading
case affirmatively answering this question. According to the
Wachauf Case, human rights 'requirements are also binding
on the Member States when they implement Community rules'.
The case concerned a German farmer who was threatened with
losing Community compensation for the discontinuance of
milk production (→ *10.5*) as a result of the specifics of German
implementing legislation of a Community regulation (→*4.6*). In
a preliminary ruling the ECJ:

> observed that Community rules which, upon the expiry
> of the lease, had the effect of depriving the lessee,
> without compensation, of the fruits of his labour and
> of his investments in the tenanted holding would be

incompatible with the requirements of the protection of fundamental rights in the Community legal order. Since those requirements are also binding on the Member States when they implement Community rules, the Member States must, as far as possible, apply those rules in accordance with those requirements.

However, according to Joined Cases 60 and 61/84 *Cinéthèque* v. *Fédération Nationale des Cinémas Français* [1985] ECR 2605, the ECJ 'has no power to examine the compatibility with the European Convention of national legislation which concerns . . . an area which falls within the jurisdiction of the national legislator'. This latter holding was affirmed in Case 12/86 *Demirel* v. *Stadt Schwäbisch Gmünd* [1987] ECR 3719, where 'national rules at issue did not have to implement a provision of Community law. In those circumstances, the Court does not have jurisdiction to determine whether national rules such as those at issue are compatible with the principles enshrined in Article 8 of the ECHR.' This clearly underlines the position that the ECJ's jurisdiction over fundamental rights cases is, in principle, limited to those with a strong Community connection.

The Court has, however, found another limited possibility of fundamental rights review of Member State action in cases of **derogations** from **Community freedoms**. In Case 260/89 *Elleniki Radiophonia Tiléorassi (ERT)* v. *Dimtiki (DEP)* [1991] ECR I-2925, it held that:

> where a Member State relies on [TEC provisions] in order to justify rules which are likely to obstruct the exercise of the freedom to provide services, such justification, provided for by Community law, must be interpreted in the light of the general principles of law and in particular of fundamental rights. Thus, the national rules in question can fall under the exceptions provided for by the combined provisions of Articles [46 and 55 TEC] only

if they are compatible with the fundamental rights the observance of which is ensured by the Court.

In Case C-112/00 *Schmidberger* v. *Austria* [2003] ECR I-5659, the ECJ reaffirmed that the protection of fundamental rights 'justified a restriction of the obligations imposed by Community law, even under a fundamental freedom guaranteed by the Treaty such as the free movement of goods' (→ 7.7). In the particular case, it found that the permission given to hold a demonstration against the environmental danger stemming from trans-Alpine road traffic, which implied the temporary closure of transit roads between Italy and Austria did not violate the free movement of goods. The ECJ held that the measures taken to ensure the freedom of expression and assembly were limited, necessary and proportionate.

6.14 Does Community law provide for 'sanctions' against Member States for human rights violations?

In general, the human rights performance of EU Member States is a matter of compliance with the ECHR and is supervised by the ECtHR in Strasbourg. The EU's fundamental rights policy, on the other hand, is aimed at acts of EU institutions (→6.2) and only exceptionally addresses the actions of Member States, as in the case of implementing measures (→ 6.13).

The Amsterdam Treaty inserted, however, a very broad fundamental rights commitment into the EU Treaty. According to Article 6(1) TEU:

> The Union is founded on the principles of liberty, democracy, respect for human rights and fundamental freedoms, and the rule of law, principles which are common to the Member States.

At the same time a new provision was inserted into Article 7 TEU, whereby:

> the Council, meeting in the composition of the Heads of State or Government and acting by unanimity on a proposal by one third of the Member States or by the Commission and after obtaining the consent of the European Parliament, may determine the existence of a **serious and persistent breach** by a **Member State** of principles mentioned above.

If such a determination were made, the Council, acting by a qualified majority, could decide to **suspend** certain **rights** devolved to the Member State in question by virtue of the Treaty. In so doing, it would take into account the possible consequences of such a suspension on the rights and obligations of natural and legal persons. To date, however, no such action has been taken and it remains doubtful whether this suspension power will ever be invoked because of its highly disruptive potential.

6.15 What is the Charter of Fundamental Rights of the EU?

In 1999, the Cologne European Council decided to commission the drafting of a **Charter of Fundamental Rights for the EU** in order to 'make their overriding importance and relevance more visible to the Union's citizens'. This task was carried out by a **'Convention'**, an ad hoc body composed of representatives of various constituent bodies, such as the European institutions, national parliaments and the heads of state or government of the Member States. In a relatively transparent and participatory procedure, this Convention **drafted** the text of the **Charter**. The Fundamental Rights Charter basically contains the rights found in the ECHR, as well as in other more recent human rights instruments and in national constitutions. They are grouped into six chapters, entitled as follows: I. – dignity; II. – freedoms; III. – equality; IV. – solidarity; V. – citizen's rights; and VI. – justice. While the traditional civil and political rights are mostly found in Chapter II, some of the more controversial social and economic guarantees are contained in Chapter III.

The Fundamental Rights Charter was 'solemnly proclaimed' by the Commission, the Council and the Parliament and approved by the Member States at the **Nice European Council** in December 2000. Clearly this falls short of being legally binding.

The ECJ's advocates-general as well as the CFI have been quick, however, to rely on the Charter's **persuasive authority**, while the ECJ itself has remained more cautious. Only in 2006, in Case C-540/03 *European Parliament* v. *Council* [2006] ECR I-5769 and in Case C-131/03P *Reynolds Tobacco* v. *Commission* [2006] ECR I-7795, did the ECJ start to refer approvingly to the Fundamental Rights Charter as a reaffirmation of the existing case law. Article I-9(1) of the **Draft Constitution Treaty** would have integrated the Fundamental Rights Charter into the EU Treaty combined with the still rather weak formulation according to which 'the Union shall recognise the rights, freedoms, and principles set out in the Charter of Fundamental Rights which constitutes Part II'. After the rejection of the **Lisbon Reform Treaty**, which would have also incorporated the Fundamental Rights Charter, the latter remains a highly persuasive **source of inspiration** for the Community institutions, in particular the **European courts**.

7 The free movement of goods

Gradually establishing the free movement of goods, one of the **four freedoms** of the internal market, was one of the centre-pieces of early market integration in the EEC. This was pursued by **internal** and **external measures**. Article 9(1) of the original 1957 EEC Treaty (now Article 23(1) TEC) provided for the gradual establishment of a **customs union** between the Member States and a **common customs tariff** vis-à-vis third countries.

Internally, a customs union requires the elimination of **customs duties** and 'charges having equivalent effect' (Article 25 TEC) as well as of discriminatory or protectionist **internal taxes** (Article 90 TEC), plus the elimination of **quantitative restrictions** on imports and exports and 'measures having equivalent effect' (Articles 28 and 29 TEC).

Externally, the **Common Customs Tariff** is fixed by EC legislation in the form of Council regulations, which have been regularly updated since 1968. The Common Customs Tariff forms part of the Community's exclusive powers in the field of the **Common Commercial Policy**.

However, the establishment of a true internal market for goods freely circulating within the entire area of the EU was not only a 'legislative' task, pursued by rule-making through treaty norms as well as secondary **legislation** in the form of harmonisation directives and regulations. To a large extent, the common market is the 'product' of the ECJ. The Court has pushed forward market integration in a line of landmark cases, such as *Dassonville* and *Cassis de Dijon*, in which it broadly interpreted the Treaty notion of 'measures having equivalent effect', and deduced a duty of 'mutual recognition' of goods lawfully produced and marketed in any of the Member States of the EU. The combined effect of these and subsequent ECJ cases has been a considerable **limitation** of the **power of Member States** to maintain rules which could exclude the goods of other Member States from their national markets. However, the Court has not been insensitive to criticism from the national level and proved in cases such as *Keck* that it was willing to restore, at least to some extent, the autonomous **rule-making power** of **Member States**.

This chapter provides an overview of the TEC rules on the free movement of goods, as well as the ECJ's relevant case law in its historical evolution. It thereby illustrates that EU law is to a considerable extent judicially made and reflective of the inherent tension between market integration and the preservation of national peculiarities. It, thus, also mirrors the broader constitutional question as to whether the **appropriate level of regulation** is on the European or on the Member State level.

? 7.1 Explain the difference between a free trade agreement, a customs union, a common market and an economic and monetary union

These are all different forms of regional economic integration organisations which, if formed by GATT/WTO members, have to fulfil certain conditions under Article XXIV of the GATT, such as covering substantially all trade and not increasing the total burden to external trade.

In a **free trade agreement** the participating states agree to **eliminate all customs duties** among themselves. However, they retain their **autonomous external trade policy** towards third

countries, particularly their own customs duties. This necessi-
tates a (rather costly) system determining where imports originate in order to apply the correct customs rate for the particular
country of destination for the imported goods. Rules of origin
help in making this assessment.

A **customs union** makes the additional step of adopting one
common external customs tariff.

The **internal market** also comprises other **factors of production**, in the terminology of the EC other 'freedoms', namely
the **free movement of persons, services and capital.** According
to Article 14 TEC, 'the internal market shall comprise an area
without internal frontiers in which the free movement of goods,
persons, services and capital is ensured in accordance with the
provisions of this Treaty'.

A **common market**, although not defined in the TEC, is
usually considered to refer to the **internal market** plus other
common policies, such as competition, agriculture, or the
environment.

Finally, in an **economic and monetary union** economic policy
becomes 'communitarised' and a **single currency** is adopted.

7.2 What is a charge equivalent to a customs duty?

While it is relatively clear what a **customs duty** is and while
the EC Member States – in a relatively disciplined fashion
and even ahead of schedule – complied with the TEC requirement to gradually eliminate them over a twelve-year period,
the question of what exactly constituted a **charge equivalent
to a customs duty** repeatedly troubled the ECJ. Obviously, it
was too tempting for states to influence trade by these alternative tools, requiring, for instance, export levies in order to
collect statistical data, art export charges to prevent the sale of

national cultural treasures and the like. Today, Article 25 TEC unequivocally provides:

> Customs duties on imports and exports and charges having equivalent effect shall be prohibited between Member States. This prohibition shall also apply to customs duties of a fiscal nature.

It did not take the ECJ very long to adopt a strict test laying down a very **broad definition** of what is prohibited as a charge equivalent to a customs duty. In Case 24/68 *Commission* v. *Italy* [1969] ECR 193, the ECJ held that:

> **any pecuniary charge**, however small and whatever its designation and mode of application, which is **imposed unilaterally** on domestic or foreign goods **by reason of** the fact that they **cross a frontier**; and which is not a customs duty in the strict sense, constitutes a charge having equivalent effect within the meaning of Articles 9 and 12 of the Treaty, **even if** it is **not** imposed for the **benefit** of the State, is **not discriminatory** or **protective** in effect or if the product on which the charge is imposed is **not** in **competition** with any domestic product.

This standard was relied upon in Cases 2 and 3/69 *Sociaal Fonds voor de Diamantarbeiders* v. *SA Ch. Brachfeld & Sons* [1969] ECR 211, where the Court held that the payment of 0.33% of the value of imported uncut diamonds as contribution to a social benefit fund was an unlawful charge having equivalent effect.

In the *First Art Treasures Case*, Case 7/68 *Commission* v. *Italy* [1968] ECR 428, the ECJ had already determined that the qualification as a charge having equivalent effect depended only upon the **effect of the charge**, **not** on its **purpose**. In that case, the Court was of the opinion that the purpose of an Italian art export charge, which was, arguably, non-fiscal, and rather aimed at the protection of national art heritage, was irrelevant. Instead, its effect (a pecuniary burden levied on the crossing of a border) made it *per se* unlawful. In the same case the Court made the important incidental finding that art treasures are also goods covered by the Treaty provisions on the free movement of goods, since they can be valued in money and are capable of forming the subject of commercial transactions.

The irrelevance of the non-fiscal purpose of a charge due upon goods crossing an intra-Community border was reaffirmed in Case 87/75 *Bresciani* v. *Amministrazione delle Finanze* [1976] ECR 129, where the Court also prohibited charges for veterinary and public health inspections, which implied that these have to be borne by society at large (→ *4.11*).

The only exception applies in situations where Community law itself requires such inspections. In Case 18/87 *Commission* v. *Germany* [1988] ECR 5427, the Court held that veterinary inspection costs did not constitute unlawful charges having equivalent effect if they reflected the actual cost, the inspection was obligatory and prescribed by Community law and ultimately promoted the free movement of goods.

? 7.3 Outline the facts and significance of the Dassonville judgment

In **Directive 70/50**, which was applicable during the transitional period leading to the establishment of a Common Market, the Commission had already listed a number of measures by which states discriminated against imported goods and which were to be considered contrary to **Article 28 TEC**, providing that 'quantitative restrictions on imports and all measures having equivalent effect shall be prohibited between Member States'. The measures listed included minimum or maximum prices for imported products, less favourable payment conditions for imports, special conditions with regard to size, packaging, composition, identification for imported goods and others. The directive only reluctantly referred to rules that were not discriminatory on their face. While the extension to such 'indistinctly applicable rules' was clearly expressed in the *Cassis* Case (→ *7.5*), the *Dassonville* Case had already laid the groundwork for this development.

Case 8/74 *Procureur du Roi* v. *Dassonville* [1974] ECR 837 is still the leading case providing a workable definition of **'measures having equivalent effect'** according to Article 28 TEC. In this judgment the Court held that:

> All trading rules enacted by Member States which are capable of hindering, directly or indirectly, actually or potentially, intra-Community trade are to be considered as measures having an effect equivalent to quantitative restrictions.

In this particular case, a Belgian importer was fined for violating Belgian law which required whisky importers to provide a certificate of authenticity from the country of origin (Scotland) and not only from the country of direct import (France). The ECJ considered that this constituted an unreasonable hindrance to intra-Community trade.

? 7.4 Are there measures other than state laws, regulations or administrative practices that may violate Article 28 TEC?

Although the *Dassonville* formula speaks of 'trading rules enacted by Member States' it was quickly recognised that these should not be limited to statutes or other formal law. ECJ practice clearly also covers **regulatory measures** and **administrative practices**. However, the Court went beyond even that in the so-called *Buy Irish* Case, Case 249/87 *Commission* v. *Ireland* [1982] ECR 4005, where the ECJ qualified a **publicity campaign** promoting 'guaranteed Irish products' of the Irish Goods Council, a private company, as a measure having equivalent effect. In the Court's eyes it was crucial that the promoting agency **received public funding** and that there was state **influence on its management** in order to consider its activities as national practice. The ECJ sweepingly declared that 'even measures adopted by the government of a Member State which do not have binding effect may be capable of influencing the conduct of traders and consumers in that State and thus of frustrating the aims of the Community'.

In the so-called *Spanish Strawberries* Case, Case C-265/95 *Commission* v. *France* [1997] ECR I-6959, the ECJ stunned many observers by holding France responsible for the damage done by angry French farmers blockading roads against agricultural imports from Spain. The Court held that France had violated Articles 28 and 10 TEC by **not taking sufficient measures** to **prevent** the farmers from disrupting agricultural imports.

7.5 What is the Cassis formula?

The *Cassis* **Case**, short for its – to most non-German speakers unpronounceable – official name Case 120/78 *REWE Zentral AG* v. *Bundesmonopolverwaltung für Branntwein* [1979] ECR 649, is one of the cornerstones of the EC's free movement law. There are two main lessons to be drawn from that case, which involved the French blackcurrant liqueur, *Cassis de Dijon* (together with champagne – a crucial ingredient for *Kir Royal*).

First, *Cassis* states the principle of **mutual recognition** which was re-formulated in a 1980 policy communication of the EC Commission in the following words:

> Any **product lawfully produced** and **marketed** in one **Member State** must, in principle, be **admitted** to the market of **any other Member State.**

Second, *Cassis* stands for a broadening of the permissible **grounds** to **derogate** from the **free movement obligations**. This is, of course, conditional upon the fact that Community law has not developed appropriate rules in the area concerned, which in effect means that there is no harmonisation by secondary Community law. In such situations Member States may enact **'reasonable'** and **'proportionate'** regulations to ensure that the public is not harmed. The court held that:

> obstacles to movement within the Community resulting from disparities between the national laws relating to the marketing of the products in question must be accepted insofar as those provisions may be recognized as being necessary in order to satisfy **mandatory requirements** relating in particular to the effectiveness of fiscal supervision, the protection of public health, the fairness of commercial transactions and the defence of the consumer.

In this particular case, the ECJ held that a German minimum alcoholic content rule for beverages was not a reasonable measure. The Germans had unsuccessfully argued that public health and consumer protection considerations could justify the prohibition of marketing French fruit liqueur containing less alcohol than comparable German liqueurs on the grounds that this could eventually lead Germans to increased alcohol consumption and mislead them as to the liqueur's alcohol content.

7.6 For what reasons may the principle of free movement of goods be restricted?

After *Cassis*, the law has become relatively clear on this matter. On the one hand, there are the **Treaty provisions** expressly derogating from the general prohibition of quantitative restrictions and measures having equivalent effect. They are stated in Article 30 TEC:

> The provisions of Articles 28 and 29 shall not preclude prohibitions or restrictions on imports, exports or goods in transit justified on grounds of **public morality, public policy or public security**; the protection of **health and life** of humans, animals or plants; the protection of **national treasures possessing artistic, historic or archaeological value**; or the protection of **industrial and commercial property**. Such prohibitions or restrictions shall not, however, constitute a means of **arbitrary discrimination** or a **disguised restriction** on trade between Member States.

On the other hand, there are the 'mandatory requirements' of *Cassis* 'relating in particular to the **effectiveness of fiscal supervision**, the **protection of public health**, the **fairness of commercial transactions** and the **defence of the consumer**' which – if applied in a non-discriminatory and reasonable fashion – may also justify a derogation from the free movement obligations 'in the absence of common rules' (→ *7.5*).

Subsequent cases have added further 'mandatory requirements' in the sense of *Cassis*, such as **environmental protection** in Case 302/86 *Commission* v. *Denmark* [1988] ECR 4607 (→ *10.11*), **pluralism of the press** in Case C-368/95 *Vereinigte Familiapress* v. *Heinrich Bauer Verlag* [1997] ECR I-3689, the **health and safety of workers** in Case 155/80 *Oebel* [1981] ECR 1993, and the **promotion of culture** and fostering certain forms of art in Cases 60 and 61/84 *Cinéthèque* v. *Fédération Nationale des Cinémas Français* [1985] ECR 2605.

7.7 Is there also a role for fundamental rights?

The ECJ has also taken into account potential clashes between the protection of fundamental rights by Member States (→*ch. 6*) and the demands of the unrestricted free movement of goods. In Case C-112/00 *Schmidberger* v. *Austria* [2003] ECR I-5659, the Court held that the protection of **fundamental rights** 'justified a **restriction** of the obligations imposed by Community law, even under a fundamental freedom guaranteed by the Treaty such as the free **movement of goods**' (→6.13, 8.19). The case concerned a blockade of the trans-Alpine traffic routes in Austria by demonstrators expressing their concern over the environmental impact of unrestricted road traffic. The demonstrations were officially permitted by the Austrian authorities. This made the ensuing constraint on intra-Community trade clearly attributable to the Austrian government under the *Spanish Strawberries* Case doctrine (→ 7.4). However, the ECJ found a justification of the measures in the freedom of expression and assembly. Since the permissions to hold the demonstration were limited, necessary and proportionate there was no violation of the free movement of goods.

? 7.8 Is the so-called German purity law of 1516 which requires beer to be manufactured only from malted barley, hops, yeast and water consistent with Community law?

The *German Beer* Case, Case 178/84 *Commission* v. *Germany* [1987] ECR 1227, exemplifies the *Cassis* rule on mandatory requirements at work (→ 7.5). Pursuant to the German Beer Duty Act 1952, which was in turn based on a venerable statute of the early sixteenth century, only products manufactured according to the **'purity law'**, that is, without any artificial additives, could be marketed under the term 'beer'. According to the ECJ, this clearly constituted a **measure having equivalent** effect which, openly defying the principle of mutual recognition as enunciated in *Cassis*, was inconsistent with EC law.

The Court went on to address the justifications raised by the German government. The consumer protection argument, according to which German beer consumers had to be protected because they associated 'beer' exclusively with purely produced beverages, was rejected by the ECJ as disproportionate. In the Court's eyes, labelling requirements would have been sufficient to inform consumers about the content of a product.

In addition to the purity law, the German Foodstuffs Act 1974 prohibited the marketing of beer containing additives. The Court, in principle, upheld the right of Member States – in the absence of harmonisation – to decide what degree of protection of the health and life of humans they intended to assure. Such a public health justification was, however, subject to a rule of proportionality. The Court could not be persuaded that there was indeed a long-term risk to public health from additives, and found that the absence of any provisions permitting additives meeting a technological need rendered the German legislation disproportionate.

7.9 Is a Member State entitled to forbid the importation of 'indecent and obscene articles' from other Member States?

In its first reference for a preliminary ruling from the ECJ, the House of Lords wanted to know whether a total ban on the importation of sex films into the UK could be justified under Article 30 TEC. In Case 34/79 *R.* v. *Henn and Darby* [1979] ECR 3795, the ECJ held that not only 'limitations' but also a **total import ban** constituted a **'quantitative restriction'**, but that such a restriction was **justified** 'on the grounds of **public morality**' because 'it is for each Member State to determine in accordance with its own scale of values and in the form selected by it the requirements of public morality in its territory'.

What remained problematic with this ruling was the fact that different standards applied within the UK insofar as that there was no absolute ban on the possession of the items in question. This latter aspect was crucial to the different outcome in a similar, subsequent case. In Case 121/85 *Conegate Ltd* v. *Customs and Excise Commissioners* [1986] ECR 1007, involving the seizure of inflatable erotic dolls imported from Germany to the UK, the ECJ held that 'a Member State may not rely on grounds of public morality to prohibit the importation of goods from other Member States when its legislation contains no prohibition on the manufacture or marketing of the same goods on its territory'. In other words, this import ban was considered to constitute an arbitrary discrimination or protectionism contrary to Article 30, 2nd sentence TEC in view of the absence of comparably strict rules against similar domestic articles ($\rightarrow$ *7.6*).

7.10 Are national retail sales restrictions on Sundays, which lead to a demonstrable reduction of imports from other Member States, compatible with Community law?

After *Dassonville* and *Cassis*, the ECJ seemed to be willing to extend the prohibition of Article 28 TEC to virtually any (even non-discriminatory) rules which affected trade in some negative way.

The so-called **Sunday trading** cases provide a good example of the potential scope of 'measures having equivalent effect' in which it was repeatedly argued that national laws prohibiting retail sales on Sundays and public holidays reduced the total sales volume, including the sale of imported goods from other Member States. In Case 145/88 *Torfaen Borough Council* v. *B & Q plc* [1989] ECR 3851, the Court, with apparent uneasiness, accepted this premise and held in rather cryptic language that:

> Article [28 TEC] must be interpreted as meaning that the
> prohibition which it lays down does not apply to national
> rules prohibiting retailers from opening their premises on
> Sunday where the restrictive effect on Community trade
> which may result therefrom do not exceed the effects
> intrinsic to rules of this kind.

It reached this conclusion by finding a justification in the *Cassis*
sense, holding that:

> [Sunday trading rules] reflect certain political and
> economic choices in so far as their purpose is so
> arranged as to accord with national or regional socio-
> cultural characteristics, and that, in the present state of
> Community law, is a matter for Member States.

To arrive at this Community law blessing the Court relied on
its earlier decision in Case 155/80 *Oebel* [1981] ECR 1993, where
it had held that 'national rules governing hours of work, delivery and sale for bakers constitute a legitimate part of economic
and social policy consistent with the objectives of public interest pursued by the Treaty'.

Following the *Torfaen* approach, a Sunday closing requirement was upheld as **proportionate** and lawful in Joined Cases
C-306/88, 304/90 and 169/91 *Council of the City of Stoke-on-
Trent* v. *B & Q plc* [1992] ECR I-6457, and in Case C-312/89
Union Département des Syndicats CGT de l'Aisne v. *Conforama*
[1991] ECR I-997, where a French Labour Code requirement
providing for Sunday as a day of rest for employees was upheld
as protecting an imperative social interest.

7.11 What was new in the Keck case?

Although the *Sunday trading* cases and others have demonstrated the ECJ's willingness to accept certain justifications for

national rules regulating the marketing of goods, the implicit message that these rules were, in principle, considered to constitute measures prohibited by Article 28 TEC did not make the Member States very happy.

For them relief came in the form of an important case which was transferred from chamber to plenary proceedings, and which is generally considered as having partly **overruled** *Dassonville* and *Cassis*. In a preliminary ruling in Joined Cases C-267 and 268/91 *Criminal Proceedings against Keck and Mithouard* [1993] ECR I-6097, the Court held that **'selling arrangements'**, or better **'marketing modalities'**, which are applied **indiscriminately** to all traders were **not** to be regarded as **'measures having equivalent effect'** in the sense of *Dassonville*. Keck and Mithouard were prosecuted in French courts for re-selling goods at a loss which was contrary to a French law. The ECJ recognised the correlation to the *Sunday trading* cases invoked by Keck and Mithouard in order to characterise the prohibition on resale at a loss as an unlawful measure having equivalent effect. It found that such legislation might restrict the volume of sales and hence the volume of sales of products from other Member States. It hastened to add, however, that it remained unclear 'whether such a possibility is sufficient to characterize the legislation in question as a measure having equivalent effect'. In this respect the Court came to a negative answer:

> However, contrary to what has previously been decided,
> the application to products from other Member States
> of national provisions restricting or prohibiting certain
> selling arrangements is not such as to hinder directly or
> indirectly, actually or potentially, trade between Member
> States within the meaning of the *Dassonville* judgment,
> provided that those provisions apply to all affected
> traders operating within the national territory and
> provided that they affect in the same manner, in law and

in fact, the marketing of domestic products and of those
from other Member States.

Where those conditions are fulfilled, the application
of such rules to the sale of products from another
Member State meeting the requirements laid down
by that State is not by nature such as to prevent their
access to the market or to impede access any more than
it impedes the access of domestic products. Such rules
therefore fall outside the scope of Article [28] of the
Treaty.

It should not come as a surprise that in the post-*Keck* phase,
in Joined Cases C-69 and 258/93 *Punto Casa* v. *Sindaco del
Comune di Capena* [1994] ECR I-2355, Italian **Sunday closing
rules** were held to fall outside the scope of Article 28 TEC.
Other **'selling arrangements'** that were covered by the new *Keck*
rule concerned an **advertising prohibition** of a pharmacists'
association in Case C-292/92 *Hünermund* v. *Landesapotheker
Baden-Württemberg* [1993] ECR I-6787, **shop opening hours** in
Joined Cases C-401 and 402/92 *Criminal Proceedings against
Tankstation 't Heukske vof and J.B.E. Boermans* [1994] ECR
I-2199 and **restrictions on places** where tobacco could be **sold**
in Case C-387/93 *Banchero* [1995] ECR I-4663.

Subsequent cases have also shown that the **distinction**
between **'product requirements'** and **'selling arrangements'** is
not always easy to draw. Some marketing restrictions, in particular for consumer protection reasons, are so closely related
to the products in question that they have been considered
under Article 28 TEC. In Case C-470/93 *Verein gegen Unwesen
in Handel und Gewerbe Köln* v. *Mars* [1995] ECR I-1923, the ECJ
held that German Unfair Competition Law rules which prohibited the sale of ice cream bars with a logo on them saying '+10%'
was held to hinder intra-Community trade because it 'may
compel the importer to adjust the presentation of his product

according to the place where they are to be marketed and consequently to incur additional packaging and advertising costs.' Similarly, in Case C-315/92 *Verband Sozialer Wettbewerb* v. *Clinique Laboratories* [1994] ECR I-317, it was the dual burden of regulation both in the state of production as well as the state of sale which made the German ban on the use of the word 'clinique' for cosmetics an unlawful measure under Article 28 TEC.

The line between 'product requirements' and 'selling arrangements' was further blurred by Case C-189/95 *Criminal Proceedings against Franzén* [1997] ECR I-5909, in which the ECJ held that the Swedish licensing system for wholesalers importing alcoholic beverages, apparently a 'selling arrangement', was contrary to Article 28 TEC. According to the Court, the highly restrictive system 'constitutes an obstacle to the importation of alcoholic beverages from other Member States in that it imposes additional costs on such beverages, such as intermediary costs, payment of charges and fees or the grant of a licence, and costs rising from the obligation to maintain storage capacity in Sweden'.

? 7.12 What is the role of the tax provision of Article 90 TEC in the context of free movement of goods?

Article 90 TEC provides:

> No Member State shall impose directly, on the products of other Member States any internal taxation of any kind in excess of that imposed directly or indirectly on similar domestic products.
>
> Furthermore, no Member State shall impose on the products of other Member States any internal taxation of such a nature as to afford indirect protection to other products.

This prohibition of **discriminatory** or **protective internal taxation** complements the Treaty's provisions on the elimination of customs duties and charges having equivalent effect in order to ensure undistorted free movement of goods within the EC's internal market. While Article 25 TEC prohibits duties or charges collected as a result of goods crossing a border ($\rightarrow$ *7.2*), Article 90 TEC outlaws internal fiscal discrimination once goods have entered a particular Member State.

In its case law as exemplified in Case 45/75 *REWE* v. *Hauptzollamt Landau/Pfalz* [1976] ECR 181, the ECJ has clarified that similarity in the sense of Article 90 TEC does not require identity but rather refers to goods which 'have similar characteristics and meet the same needs from the point of view of the consumer'. Applied to the unavoidable field of alcoholic products, the Court struck down a number of national tax regimes providing for different tax rates for different kinds of spirits. For instance, in Case 168/78 *Commission* v. *France* [1980] ECR 347, the Court found that a 'characteristic of [the French tax] system is in fact that an essential part of domestic production . . . spirits obtained from wine and fruit, come within the most favourable tax category whereas at least two types of product, almost all of which are imported from other Member States, are subject to higher taxation'. As the Cases 169/78 *Commission* v. *Italy* [1980] ECR 409, and 171/78 *Commission* v. *Denmark* [1980] ECR 447 demonstrate, France was not the only Member State engaging in such a practice.

The ECJ clarified that Article 90(1) TEC prohibits both **direct** and **indirect discrimination**. In Case 112/84 *Humblot* v. *Directeur des Services Fiscaux* [1985] ECR 1367, the Court had to assess the legality of a French car tax system which depended upon the power rating of the cars. It held that 'although the system embodies no formal distinction based on the origin of the products it manifestly exhibits discriminatory or protective features contrary to Article [90], since the power rating determining liability to the special tax has been fixed at a level such that only imported cars, in particular from other Member States, are subject to the special tax whereas all cars of domestic manufacture are liable to the distinctly more advantageous differential tax'. The ECJ made clear, however, that differential car tax rates may be compatible with Article 90 TEC if they serve, for instance, **environmental purposes**. In Case C-132/88 *Commission* v. *Greece* [1990] ECR I-1567, the Court held that this objective justification can be upheld even where imported cars only fall into the highest tax category.

In Case 170/78 *Commission* v. *United Kingdom* [1983] ECR 2265, the Court had to deal with a tax regime that imposed an excise tax on wine that was roughly five times higher than that for beer. Though the Court did not consider the two alcoholic products to be sufficiently similar in order to consider the UK practice under Article 90(1) TEC, it found a violation of Article 90(2) TEC because the 'United Kingdom's tax system has the effect of subjecting wine imported from other Member States to an additional burden so as to afford protection to domestic beer production.'

The precise distinction between Article 90(1), prohibiting discriminatory taxation of 'similar' goods, and Article 90(2) TEC, prohibiting 'protective' taxation against imported goods which may compete with domestic goods, is not always easy to draw. Thus, in the abovementioned Case 168/78 *Commission* v. *France* [1980] ECR 347, the ECJ found that the French alcohol tax system, imposing rather high taxes on grain-based spirits, such as rum, gin, whisky and vodka, while providing for rather low taxes for fruit-based spirits, such as armagnac, calvados and cognac, also had a protective effect contrary to Article 90(2) TEC.

8 The free movement of persons

In addition to the effective implementation of the **free movement of goods**, characteristic of a customs union, the Community has always aimed at guaranteeing the **free movement of persons** in order to create a true internal market. This 'internal market' is defined in Article 14(2) TEC as 'an area without internal borders in which the free movement of goods, persons, services and capital is ensured'. The history of the EC/EU is the history of the gradual implementation of these so-called **four freedoms** which follows a similar regulatory pattern, that is, **ensuring non-discrimination** and **eliminating intra-Community restrictions** by Member States.

This chapter will provide an overview on the Community rules on the free movement of natural and legal persons, that is, individuals and companies. They originate in three sets of Treaty provisions: **the free movement of 'workers'**; the **freedom of establishment**; and the **freedom to provide services**. The resulting, rather narrow economic rights have been broadened through the case law of the ECJ and secondary Community legislation, which has almost led to a **general right of free movement**. The Luxembourg Court did so by broadly interpreting the entitlements contained in Treaty provisions and by gradually restricting the powers of Member States to limit these rights.

❓ 8.1 Is there a general right to free movement for all EU citizens?

The Maastricht Treaty introduced the concept of **Community citizenship** which, according to Article 17 TEC, **derives** from and **complements** the **nationality** of the **Member States**.

Although Article 18 TEC broadly stipulates that 'every **citizen of the Union** shall have the **right** to **move and reside freely within the territory of the Member States**', one should not overlook the *caveat* that any such right is '**subject to** the **limitations** and conditions laid down in this Treaty and by the measures adopted to give it effect'. In reality, therefore, the right of free movement and residence remains dependent upon availing oneself of economic rights either as a worker or as a self-employed person or other EC entitlements.

The precise conditions of the **free movement rights of workers** are laid down in **Article 39 TEC** as follows:

(1) **Freedom of movement for workers** shall be secured within the Community.

(2) Such freedom of movement shall entail the **abolition** of any **discrimination** based on nationality between workers of the Member States as regards employment, remuneration and other conditions of work and employment.

(3) It shall entail the right, subject to limitations justified on grounds of public policy, public security or public health:

    (a) to **accept offers of employment** actually made;

    (b) to **move freely within the territory** of Member States **for this purpose**;

    (c) to **stay** in a Member State **for the purpose of employment** in accordance with the provisions governing the employment of nationals of that State laid down by law, regulation or administrative action;

(d) to **remain** in the territory of a Member State **after
having been employed** in that State, subject to
conditions which shall be embodied in implementing
regulations to be drawn up by the Commission.

(4) The provisions of this Article shall **not** apply to
employment in the **public service**.

In addition, the Community has adopted a wide range of
secondary legislation based on Article 40 TEC, which provides
that the Council shall 'acting in accordance with the procedure
referred to in Article 251 and after consulting the Economic and
Social Committee, issue directives or make regulations setting out
the measures required to bring about freedom of movement for
workers, as defined in Article 39 . . .' (→3.7). The most important
early legislative acts are: Directive 64/221 on public policy, security and health derogations (→8.9); Directive 68/360 on entry and
residence requirements of workers and their families; Regulation
1612/68, which contains several core rights of workers and their
family members (→ 8.4, 8.6–8); and Regulation 1251/70 on the
right to remain in another Member State after employment.

Rights of residence of persons **other than workers** or self-
employed persons have been accepted by the Member States
only reluctantly. In the 1990s a number of directives conferred
such rights on persons who had ceased to work (Directive
90/365), students exercising the right to vocational training
(Directive 90/366, replaced by Directive 93/96) and others,
such as the so-called 'Playboy' Directive 90/364 which gave
free movement rights also to persons not participating in any
economic activity as long as they could afford their expenses.
According to all these directives, however, **residence rights**
were **dependent** upon the **availability of adequate resources** so
as not to become a burden on the social assistance schemes of
the Member States and sickness insurance coverage.

Most of these acts have been replaced by **Directive 2004/38 on the Rights of Citizens of the Union and their Family Members to Move and Reside Freely within the Territory of the Member States,** which had to be implemented by April 2006 (→ *8.6–9*). This harmonised the existing, rather fragmented, law, although Article 14(1) retained the basic idea that residence rights of EU citizens 'must not become an unreasonable burden on the public finances of the host Member State', as the ECJ had expressed in Case C-413/99 *Baumbast* v. *Secretary of State for the Home Department* [2002] ECR I-7091.

8.2 Who is a 'worker' benefiting from the free movement rights enshrined in the Treaty and secondary EC law?

In general, the ECJ adopted a rather **expansive interpretation** of who qualifies as a **'worker'.**

In Case 58/81 *Levin* v. *Staatssecretaris van Justitie* [1982] ECR 1035, the ECJ held that **part-time workers** could also benefit from free movement rights as long as they pursued **'effective and genuine economic activities'.** The only exclusion was work 'on such a small scale as to be regarded as purely marginal and ancillary'.

In Case 66/85 *Lawrie-Blum* v. *Land Baden Württemberg* [1986] ECR 2121, the Court considered that a trainee teacher also qualified as a worker under Article 39 TEC (→ *8.1*). It suggested the following test: 'The essential feature of an employment relationship, however, is that for a certain time a person **performs services** for and **under the direction** of another person in return for which he receives **remuneration.'** In Case 196/87 *Steymann* v. *Staatssecretaris van Justitie* [1988] ECR 6159, the ECJ held that even 'unpaid work' for a religious community (Bhaghwan) was 'work', since remuneration existed in the form of the religious community's obligation to provide for the material needs of its members. In Case C-456/02 *Trojani* v. *CPAS* [2004] ECR I-7573, the Court confirmed that 'activities cannot be regarded as real and genuine economic activity if they constitute merely a means of rehabilitation or reintegration for the persons concerned'. It cautioned, however, that services performed by a former drug addict in the course of a reintegration programme could constitute 'work' if they were 'capable of being regarded as forming part of the normal labour market'.

Although not fully qualifying as workers, the ECJ has expansively interpreted the TEC provisions for the benefit of **job-seekers**. In the *Antonissen* Case, Case C-292/89 *R.* v. *Immigration Appeal Tribunal, ex parte Antonissen* [1991] ECR I-745, the Court considered that Article 39(3) TEC 'must be interpreted as enumerating, in a non-exhaustive way, certain rights benefiting nationals of Member States in the context of the free movement of workers and that that freedom also entails the right for nationals of Member States to move freely within the territory of the Member States and to stay there for the purposes of seeking employment.' However, states still retain the power to expel those who remain unsuccessful for a longer period of time.

? 8.3 Discuss the scope of the non-discrimination obligation contained in Article 39(2) TEC

It is clear that Article 39(2) TEC prohibits any **direct discrimination** on the basis of **nationality**, which may be justified only under the **'public service'** exception of Article 39(4) TEC discussed below (→ *8.10*).

Most of the practical issues arose, however, in the context of various forms of **indirect discrimination**. In this context the ECJ has traditionally been rather suspicious about various national rules that can be fulfilled more easily by nationals than non-nationals, such as **residence** or **requirements** relating to the **place of education**. Two other forms of indirect discrimination were found by the ECJ in the cases discussed below.

In Case 13/69 *Württembergische Milchverwertung-Südmilch-AG* v. *Ugliola* [1970] ECR 363, the ECJ held that German legislation, which provided that only military service in the Bundeswehr, the German army, counted as surrogate employment time for seniority, pension and job security purposes was 'indirectly introducing discrimination in favour of their own nationals alone', since service in the Bundeswehr would be satisfied by a greater number of Germans than other Community nationals. In a reverse nationality constellation, in Case C-419/92 *Scholz* v. *Universitaria di Cagliari* [1994] ECR I-505, the Court held that a job recruitment system for canteen workers, awarding points for previous employment in the Italian public sector, constituted indirect discrimination against a German worker.

? 8.4 Are language requirements for certain jobs forms of indirect discrimination contrary to EC law?

While **language requirements** are a typical form of indirect discrimination they may still be justifiable for certain jobs. Thus, Article 3(1) of Regulation 1612/68 permits the imposition of 'conditions relating to **linguistic knowledge** required **by reason of the nature of the post to be filled**'.

In Case 379/87 *Groener* v. *Minister for Education* [1989] ECR 3967, the ECJ upheld as non-discriminatory an Irish language test which was a condition of employment for a teaching post, even though Irish was not the language of instruction. The Court reasoned that the TEC did not prohibit the protection and promotion of the national language if the measures are proportionate. It has been rightly suggested that this outcome was influenced by the high political importance attached to the protection of cultural diversity and identity in the Community, and the judgment may be seen as an example of the Court reacting to strong political pressure from Member States in certain fields.

In Joined Cases C-259, 331–332/91 *Allué, Coonan and others* v. *Università degli studi di Venezia and Parma* [1993] ECR 4309, however, the ECJ found an indirect discrimination on the basis of language unjustifiable. The Court was of the opinion that different employment contracts for foreign-language assistants and other university personnel in Italy mainly disadvantaged non-Italians. In this context, it reiterated that:

> the principle of equal treatment, of which Article [39(2)] of the Treaty is one embodiment, prohibits not only overt discrimination based on nationality but all covert forms of discrimination which, by applying other distinguishing criteria, in fact achieve the same result.

8.5 Are private parties bound by the non-discrimination obligation of Article 39(2) TEC?

This is an issue similar to the question raised in the context of free movement of goods law, asking what constitutes a 'measure' in the sense of Article 28 TEC and how far activities of private parties could fall under its prohibition, which was discussed in cases such as *Buy Irish,* Case 249/87 *Commission* v. *Ireland* [1982] ECR 4005 and *Spanish Strawberries*, Case C-265/95 *Commission* v. *France* [1997] ECR I-6959 (→ 7.4).

With regard to the free movement of persons, it is discussed as the 'horizontal effect' of Article 39(2) TEC, that is, whether free movement obligations may be invoked only against a Member

State ('vertically') or also against **private parties** ('horizontally') ($\rightarrow$ 4.8). Thanks to cyclists, football and basketball players and other professional athletes, the ECJ has successively struck down as discriminatory (on the basis of nationality) the regulations of sporting associations.

In the early leading case involving Belgian speed cyclists, in Case 36/74 *Walrave & Koch* [1974] ECR 1405, the Court broadly stated that:

> Prohibition of such discrimination does not only apply to the action of public authorities but extends likewise to rules of any other nature aimed at regulating in a collective manner gainful employment and the provision of services . . .
>
> Since, moreover, working conditions in the various Member States are governed sometimes by means of provisions laid down by law or regulations and sometimes by agreements and other acts concluded or adopted by private persons, to limit the prohibitions in question to acts of a public authority would risk creating inequality in their application.

In the famous *Bosman* Case, Case C-415/93 *Union Royal Belge des Sociétés de Football Association* v. *Bosman* [1995] ECR I-4921, the ECJ found fault with the transfer system of European national and transnational football associations. It held that transfer rules which regularly involved rather large sums of money being paid to clubs in order to engage a player as constituting:

> an obstacle to freedom of movement for workers prohibited in principle by Article 48 [now Article 39] of the Treaty. It could only be otherwise if those rules pursued a legitimate aim compatible with the Treaty and were justified by pressing reasons of public interest. But even if that were so, application of those rules would still

have to be such as to ensure achievement of the aim in question and not go beyond what is necessary for that purpose.

This latter rule of reason clearly echoes the Court's reasoning in *Cassis,* Case 120/78 *REWE Zentral AG* v. *Bundesmonopolverwaltung für Branntwein* [1979] ECR 649 (→ *7.5*). At the same time, the Court rejected the suggestion to regard the transfer rules as comparable to 'selling arrangements' in the sense of *Keck,* Joined Cases C-267 and 268/91 *Criminal Proceedings against Keck and Mithouard* [1993] ECR I-6097, which would thus fall outside the scope of the free movement provisions (→ *7.11*).

The *Bosman* decision was followed in Case C-176/96 *Jyri Lehtonen and Others* v. *Fédération Royale Belge des Sociétés de Basket-ball ASBL (FRBSB)* [2000] ECR I-2681, where the Court held that rules preventing professional basketball players from taking part in competitions if they had been transferred after a certain date may constitute an obstacle to free movement of workers.

All these cases involved employers or employers' associations which had some general regulatory powers. The open question as to whether the **horizontal effect** of Article 39(2) TEC also applied to individual employers was resolved affirmatively by the ECJ in Case C-281/89 *Angonese* v. *Cassa di Risparmio di Bolzano SpA* [2000] ECR I-4139, wherein the Court said that 'the prohibition of discrimination on grounds of nationality laid down in Article 48 [now Article 39] . . . must be regarded as **applying to private persons** as well'. As a consequence, it held that the requirement of possessing a special certificate of bilingualism in order to compete for a post with a private Italian bank to be contrary to the non-discrimination rule of Article 39 TEC, since such certificates were issued by authorities only in northern Italy.

8.6 How did the ECJ interpret the crucial notion of 'social advantages' contained in the EC's free movement of workers legislation?

The Treaty not only prohibits discrimination and other obstacles to the free movement of workers, it also confers **positive rights** on EC **workers**. Many of these rights are spelled out in more detail in **secondary legislation**, the centre-piece of which has been Regulation 1612/68 on free movement of workers within the Community. Part I contained the most important provisions relating to eligibility for employment (Articles 1–6), equality of treatment within employment (Articles 7–9) and on workers' families (Articles 10–12), which are now governed by Directive 2004/38.

Article 7 Regulation 1612/68 extended the **non-discrimination** obligation of Article 39(2) TEC, which is literally limited to 'conditions of work and employment', **to social and tax issues** and to **vocational training**. In particular, the ECJ's **teleological interpretation** (*effet utile*) of Article 7(2) Regulation 1612/68, which provides that Community workers 'shall enjoy the same social and tax advantages as national workers', has broadened considerably the rights of Community workers.

The Court rejected attempts to limit the notion of social and tax benefits to those directly connected to the employment relation itself, although it insisted that the advantages had to be **connected** to the claimants' **'objective status'** as **workers**.

In Case 32/75 *Cristini (Fiorini)* v. *SNCF* [1975] ECR 1085, the ECJ held that, 'in view of the equality of treatment which the provision seeks to achieve, the substantive area of application must be delineated so as to include all social and tax advantages, whether or not attached to the contract of employment, such as reduction in fares for large families'. Thus, the refusal by the French state railway to issue such a reduced fare card to the Italian widow of an Italian worker in France was unlawful. In Case 65/81 *Reina* v. *Landeskreditbank Baden-Württemberg* [1982] ECR 33, the ECJ even qualified interest-free childbirth loans granted under German legislation to German nationals as 'social advantages' wherein no discrimination was admissible.

A certain limit to the expansive interpretation of Article 7(2) Regulation 1612/68 was drawn in Case 207/78 *Ministère Public* v. *Even* [1979] ECR 2019, in which a French national complained that a special retirement pension benefit given exclusively to Belgian Second World War veterans unlawfully discriminated against him in the field of social advantages. The ECJ, however, considered that the essential objective of the benefit in question was to give Belgian nationals 'an advantage by reason of the hardships suffered for that country', and that such a benefit 'cannot therefore be considered as an advantage granted to a national worker by reason primarily of his status of worker or resident on the national territory and for that reason does not fulfil the essential characteristics of the "social advantages" referred to in Article 7(2) of Regulation no 1612/68'. A similar logic was applied in Case C-386/02 *Baldinger* v. *Pensionsversicherungsanstalt der Arbeiter* [2004] ECR I-1417, with regard to an Austrian system of compensation payments for prisoners of war. In the Court's view, such payments, which were made to Austrian citizens only, were not linked to the recipients' status as workers but instead granted 'in testimony of national gratitude for the hardships they endured and is thus paid as a quid pro quo for the services they rendered to their country'.

Article 7(2) Regulation 1612/68 is limited to workers, it does not cover those who are self-employed. The ECJ, however, inferred social advantages of self-employed Community nationals and their families directly from Article 43 TEC, providing for the freedom of establishment (→ *8.12*). Thus, in Case C-111/91 *Commission* v. *Luxembourg* [1993] ECR I-817, a residence requirement for the entitlement to certain child allowances was considered to constitute an unjustifiable indirect discrimination contrary to both Article 7(2) Regulation 1612/68 and Article 43 TEC. With regard to social advantages, the distinction between workers and self-employed has become a moot point as a result of Article 24(1) Directive 2004/38, which provides that all EU citizens residing in another Member State shall enjoy equal treatment.

8.7 How are the rights of the family members of workers protected?

The free movement of workers would hardly be effective if it were narrowly confined to the workers themselves, in particular, if it did not include a right to be joined by the family members of those workers.

While family members are not even mentioned in the TEC, they are expressly covered by Regulation 1612/68. Most importantly, Article 10 provides:

(1) The following shall, irrespective of their nationality, have the right to install themselves with a worker who is a national of one Member State and who is employed in the territory of another Member State:

(a) his spouse and their descendants who are under the age of 21 years or are dependants;

(b) dependent relatives in the ascending line of the worker and his spouse.

(2) Member States shall facilitate the admission of any member of the family not coming within the provisions of paragraph 1 if dependent on the worker referred to above or living under his roof in the country whence he comes.

> (3) For the purposes of paragraphs 1 and 2, the worker
>   must have available for his family housing considered
>   as normal for national workers in the region where
>   he is employed; this provision, however must not give
>   rise to discrimination between national workers and
>   workers from the other Member States.

In spite of the ECJ's rather **broad approach** to the rights of
family members, continuing family links remain **important**,
especially for non-Community nationals. In Case 267/83 *Diatta*
v. *Land Berlin* [1985] ECR 567, the Court held that a Senegalese
national, who was already separated from her French husband
and wanted to divorce him, still had a right of residence in
Germany since her marital relationship had not yet been terminated. In the Court's view:

> Article 10 of the Regulation does not require that the
> member of the family in question must live permanently
> with the worker, but, as is clear from Article 10(3),
> only that the accommodation which the worker has
> available must be such as may be considered normal
> for the purpose of accommodating his family. A
> requirement that the family must live under the same
> roof permanently cannot be implied.

In addition, Article 11 gave spouses and under-aged children of
workers – even if they are not Community nationals – an independent right to employment in the host state.

Articles 10 and 11 Regulation 1612/68 have been repealed by
Directive 2004/38, which now governs the entry and residence
rights of all EU citizens. Article 2(2)(b) extends the definition
of 'family members' to include not only spouses, descendants
and certain ascendant relatives, but also partners in 'registered
partnerships' if recognised as equivalent to marriage by the
legislation of the host Member State. Directive 2004/38 is also

a typical piece of EU legislation in that it partially codifies rulings of the ECJ. A clear example is Article 13 of the directive entitled 'Retention of the right of residence by family members in the event of divorce, annulment of marriage or termination of registered partnership'. However, the Court's rather liberal approach may have been cut back by the legislator who, in Article 16(2) of the new directive, for example, provided that family members must have resided 'with the Union citizen' for five years in order to be eligible for permanent residence rights or that rights may be withdrawn in cases of abuse of rights 'such as marriages of convenience'.

? 8.8 Does EC law confer rights to education?

Though **education** is, of course, crucial for getting good jobs, it was not part of the Community's express competences until the Maastricht Treaty. Nevertheless, some **educational rights** were already included in **Community legislation** and could be derived from **general Community principles** by the ECJ. For example, Article 12 Regulation 1612/68 provided that:

> The children of a national of a Member State who is or has been employed in the territory of another Member State shall be admitted to that State's general educational, apprenticeship and vocational training courses under the same conditions as the nationals of that State, if such children are residing in its territory.
>
> Member States shall encourage all efforts to enable such children to attend these courses under the best possible conditions.

In a rather controversial ruling in Case 9/74 *Casagrande* v. *Landeshauptstadt München* [1974] ECR 733, the ECJ held that a Bavarian student grant was an issue of 'admittance to education' in the sense of Article 12, Regulation 1612/68 where no discrimination is allowed. Less controversial – because clearly in line with the text of Article 12 – was the Court's ruling in Case C-7/94 *Gaal* [1996] ECR I-1031, in which the educational rights of non-dependent children over 21 were confirmed. This resulted from the fact that Article 12 had a broader coverage than Article 10 of the Regulation (→ *8.7*).

Interestingly, the educational rights of workers themselves are narrower under Regulation 1612/68. Its Article 7(3) provides that they shall have equal access only to 'training in vocational schools and retraining centres'. Thus, the ECJ held in cases such as Case 39/86 *Lair* v. *Universität Hannover* [1981] ECR 3161 and Case 197/86 *Brown* v. *Secretary of State for Scotland* [1988] ECR 3205, that EC law did not provide general equal treatment with regard to access to and financial and other support for studying at universities, since both education and social policy were, in principle, matters within the competence of the Member States. In the *Lair* Case, the Court clarified that 'the concept of a vocational school is a more limited one and refers exclusively to institutions which provide only instruction either alternating with or closely linked to an occupational activity'.

Also the TEC's general non-discrimination clause in Article 12 TEC was used by the ECJ to further educational rights. This was particularly important for persons who could not claim the same rights as workers or as their dependants. In the famous *Gravier* Case, Case 293/83 *Gravier* v. *City of Liège* [1985] ECR 593, the Court held that a Belgian enrolment fee which was requested from a French student (but not from Belgian students) was contrary to Article 12 TEC. With its typical teleological reasoning the ECJ found the required connection of access to education with Community law in the potential effect of education on subsequent ability to find work. Thus, the case fell within the scope of the Treaty. The ECJ held that:

Access to vocational training is in particular likely
to promote free movement of persons throughout the
Community, by enabling them to obtain a qualification
in the Member State where they intend to work . . .

In Case 24/86 *Blaizot* v. *University of Liège* [1988] ECR 378,
the Court clarified that the Treaty-based non-discrimination
right was not limited to actual job-related training, but that
'vocational training' could include university education unless
it was pursued only to improve one's general knowledge.

? 8.9 Outline the major exceptions to the principle of free movement of workers as reflected in the case law of the ECJ

The public policy, public security and public health exceptions provided for in Article 39(3) TEC (→ *8.1*) have been
made more precise by Directive 64/221, now Articles 27–33
of Directive 2004/38, and have been interpreted restrictively
by the ECJ. These directives prohibit the invocation of such
grounds as 'to service economic ends' and restrict them to
grounds 'based exclusively on the personal conduct of the
individual concerned'.

The latter concept was the subject of litigation in the well-
known *Van Duyn* Case, Case 41/74 *Van Duyn* v. *Home Office*
[1974] ECR 1337 (→ *4.7*), where UK immigration authorities
refused entry and residence to a Dutch national who wanted
to work for the Church of Scientology which was considered
'socially harmful' by the UK. In a rather deferential ruling –
not in line with the Court's otherwise restrictive approach – the
ECJ found that, although membership of an organisation alone
did not constitute 'personal conduct', active participation and
identification with it would do so. The Court further held that
even though there was no prohibition on UK nationals working

for the Church of Scientology, 'the particular circumstances justifying recourse to the concept of public policy may vary from one country to another and from one period to another, and [that] it is therefore necessary in this matter to allow the competent national authorities an area of discretion within the limits imposed by the Treaty'.

This discretion was limited in Cases 115 and 116/81 *Adoui and Cornuaille* [1982] ECR 1665, where two sex workers, 'suspect from the point of view of morals', were threatened with deportation from Belgium. Although the ECJ confirmed that Community law did not provide a 'uniform scale of values as regards the assessment of conduct which may be considered as contrary to public policy', it held that:

> conduct may not be considered as being of a sufficiently serious nature to justify restrictions on the admission to or residence within the territory of a Member State of a national of another Member State in a case where the former Member State does not adopt, with respect to the same conduct on the part of its own nationals repressive measures or other genuine and effective measures intended to combat such conduct.

In Case 36/75 *Rutili* v. *Ministre de l'Intérieur* [1975] ECR 1219, the Court considered a French restriction imposed upon an Italian national to reside in certain parts of France only contrary to Article 39(3) TEC because the latter merely permitted for whole territory restrictions. Partial prohibitions were legal only if non-discriminatory according to Article 12 TEC. The Court also reaffirmed that the 'personal conduct' prerequisite under Directive 64/221 required that the 'conduct constitutes a genuine and sufficiently serious threat to public policy'.

In Case 67/74 *Bonsignore* [1975] ECR 297, the ECJ considered a German deportation order concerning an Italian national who had fatally shot his brother to be of a 'general preventive nature'. It was thus not based 'exclusively on the personal conduct of the individual concerned' and was, therefore, contrary to EC law. The Court came to a similar conclusion in Case C-348/96 *Criminal proceedings against Donatella Calfa* [1999] ECR I-11. It held that the criminal penalty of expulsion for life from the territory of one Member State of nationals of another Member State who had been found guilty of committing offences under its drug laws constituted an obstacle to the freedom to provide services and to the other fundamental freedoms guaranteed by the Treaty, which cannot be justified on grounds of public policy.

Article 29 of Directive 2004/38 ensures that public health reasons may be invoked only by Member States with regard to diseases with epidemic potential as defined by the World Health Organization.

? 8.10 Are all employees in the public service sector exempted from the rights contained in Article 39 TEC?

With regard to the public service exception provided for in Article 39(4) TEC (→ 8.1) the ECJ has consistently pursued a restrictive line of interpretation.

In Case 152/73 *Sotgiu* v. *Deutsche Bundespost* [1974] ECR 153, the Court held unequivocally that **'public service'** was a **Community notion** not open to interpretation by the Member States. It further held that Member States may restrict **admission** of foreign nationals **only** to certain activities in the public service sector, but that Article 39(4) TEC 'cannot justify discriminatory measures with regard to remuneration or other conditions of employment against workers once they have been admitted to the public service'.

Without giving a clear definition, the Court has consistently used a **restrictive** Community law **meaning,** which basically requires 'participation in the **exercise of powers** conferred by **public law**' and duties designed to safeguard the general interests of the state or of other public authorities. Typical examples of the exercise of **'official authority'** ($\rightarrow$ *8.13*) are the judiciary, the police, defence forces or tax inspectors, as was stated by the advocate-general in Case 307/84 *Commission* v. *France* [1986] ECR 1725, and as they follow *e contrario* from Commission Communication [1988] OJ C72/2, which lists public transport, utility provision, education and research as services which should be open to nationals of other Member States. Judicial examples are provided in the so-called *Belgian Public Service* Cases, Case 149/79 *Commission* v. *Belgium* [1980] ECR 3881 and [1982] ECR 1845, where the ECJ considered that, with the exception of a few posts such as city architects, night watchmen and certain supervisory posts which were regarded as exercising 'official authority', all other employment forms, such as city nurses and railway workers, did not fall under the public service exception.

8.11 Explain the issue of 'reverse discrimination'

'Reverse discrimination' is not a felicitous notion. It basically means that **Community law** does **not apply** to 'wholly internal situations'. As a result of this non-application, national workers may find themselves in a worse position than other Community nationals.

In Case 175/78 *R.* v. *Saunders* [1979] ECR 1129, the ECJ held that the applicant could not rely on Article 39 TEC to challenge an order which excluded her from part of her own territory, because there was 'no connecting factor to any situation envisaged by EC law'.

In Cases 35 and 36/82 *Morson and Jhanjan* [1982] ECR 3723, the Court ruled that two Dutch nationals working in the Netherlands could not rely on Article 10 Regulation 1612/68 (→ *8.7*) to enable them to bring their Surinamese parents into the country where they worked since they 'had never exercised the right to freedom of movement within the Community'.

In Case 180/83 *Moser* v. *Land Baden Württemberg* [1984] ECR 2539, a German citizen, who was a member of the Communist Party and was thus disadvantaged in his search for a job, could not invoke Community law vis-à-vis German hiring authorities. The Court held that a potential disadvantage in a future search for employment in another Member State was an insufficient nexus to trigger the application of Article 39 TEC.

This ruling was reaffirmed in Case C-299/95 *Kremzow* v. *Austria* [1997] ECR I-2629, concerning a former Austrian judge imprisoned in Austria for murdering a lawyer. The ECJ held that even though any deprivation of liberty might impede a person's exercise of his or her free movement rights, the purely hypothetical possibility of doing so did not entail a sufficient connection with Community law.

Reverse discrimination may be **avoided**, however, if one travels abroad in order to exercise Treaty rights. Such a **Community nexus** also helps to avoid reverse discrimination in the context of the right of establishment. Thus, in Case 115/78 *Knoors* [1979] ECR 399, a Dutch plumber with a qualification to practice in Belgium could rely thereon in order to work in the Netherlands. In Case C-370/90 *Singh* [1992] ECR I-4265, an Indian national married to a British national could claim entry and residency rights as a spouse of a Community national in the UK after they had returned from Germany where they both had been working for a number of years. Furthermore, in Case C-18/95 *Terhoeve* [1999] ECR I-345, a Dutchman successfully challenged a discriminatory Dutch social security provision after he had been employed and resided in another Member State.

? 8.12 What does the freedom of establishment guarantee?

While the rights of employees are protected by the free movement of workers, discussed above (→ 8.1–10), the economic rights of self-employed persons are guaranteed by the TEC and secondary law rules on the **freedom of establishment** and the **freedom to provide services**. As regards the former, Article 43 TEC provides that:

> Within the framework of the provisions set out below, restrictions on the freedom of establishment of nationals of a Member State in the territory of another Member State shall be prohibited. Such prohibition shall also apply to restrictions on the setting-up of agencies, branches or subsidiaries by nationals of any Member State established in the territory of any Member State.
>
> Freedom of establishment shall include the right to take up and pursue activities as self-employed persons and to set up and manage undertakings, in particular companies or firms within the meaning of the second paragraph of Article 48, under the conditions laid down for its own nationals by the law of the country where such establishment is effected, subject to the provisions of the Chapter relating to capital.

Unlike the **provision of services**, which has a more **temporary character** (→ 8.16), 'establishment' requires a 'stable and continuous basis' with the host Member State. In Case C-221/89 *R. v. Secretary of State for Transport, ex parte Factortame* [1991] ECR I-3905, the ECJ spoke of 'the actual pursuit of an economic activity through a fixed establishment in another Member State for an indefinite period'. This important judgment further clarified that local ownership requirements for the registration of a ship were contrary to the freedom of establishment.

? 8.13 Are lawyers excluded from the right of establishment because they exercise 'official authority'?

Similar to the **public service exception** provided for in the context of the free movement of workers (→ *8.1*, *8.10*), the Treaty provides in Article 45 TEC that:

> The provisions of this Chapter shall not apply, so far as any given Member State is concerned, to activities which in that State are connected, even occasionally, with the **exercise of official authority.**

In Case 2/74 *Reyners* v. *Belgium* [1974] ECR 63, the ECJ not only affirmed that the **freedom of establishment** in Article 43 had **direct effect** (→ *4.5*), it also refused to exempt the legal profession as a whole under the 'official authority' exception, thus rendering a Belgian nationality requirement for lawyers unlawful. The Court found that:

> Professional activities involving contacts, even regular and organic, with the courts, including even compulsory cooperation in their functioning, do not constitute, as such, connection with the exercise of official authority.
>
> The most typical activities of the profession of *avocat*, in particular, such as consultation and legal assistance and also representation and the defence of parties in court, even when the intervention or assistance of the *avocat* is compulsory or is a legal monopoly, cannot be considered as connected with the exercise of official authority.

? 8.14 Are non-discriminatory regulations for the exercise of the legal profession lawful under EC rules?

The text of Article 43 TEC (→ *8.12*), providing for a right of establishment 'under the conditions laid down for its own nationals', seems to prohibit direct discrimination only. In a number of cases, however, many of which have been instituted by lawyers who certainly had a fair amount of self-interest in these cases, the ECJ interpreted Article 43 TEC as prohibiting **indirect discrimination** as well.

In Case 71/76 *Thieffry* v. *Conseil de l'Ordre des Avocats à la Cour de Paris* [1977] ECR 765, the ECJ held that any restrictive qualification requirement required a 'practical benefit'. Thus, a French law degree as a prerequisite for admission to the bar, although on its face non-discriminatory, was an 'unjustified restriction' of the right of establishment where a foreign (Belgian) degree had been recognised as equivalent and where a specific professional qualifying certificate (bar exam) had been produced.

Case 107/83 *Ordre des Avocats au Bareau de Paris* v. *Klopp* [1984] ECR 2971, concerned a German lawyer who was refused admission to the Paris bar since French rules disallowed a second establishment of a lawyer outside his or her Paris chambers. The ECJ held that this rule, although non-discriminatory, violated a Community principle according to which the right of establishment 'includes the freedom to set up more than one work place in the Community', which was arguably already contained in the wording of Article 43 TEC. The Court also rejected possible justifications by holding that there were less restrictive ways of ensuring sufficient client and court contacts of lawyers and their obedience to professional rules.

In Case 340/89 *Vlassopoulou* v. *Ministerium für Justiz Baden-*

Württemberg [1991] ECR 2357, the ECJ openly addressed the indirect discrimination issue. In this case German authorities refused bar admission to a Greek national who had a Greek law degree and practised German law in Germany on the grounds that she did not have the required German exams. The Court held that:

> Even if applied without any discrimination on the basis of nationality, national requirements concerning qualifications may have the effect of hindering nationals of the other Member States in the exercise of their right of establishment . . .
>
> Consequently, a Member State which receives a request to admit a person to a profession to which access, under national law, depends upon the possession of a diploma or a professional qualification must take into consideration the diplomas, certificates and other evidence of qualifications which the person concerned has acquired in order to exercise the same profession in another Member State by making a comparison between the specialized knowledge and abilities certified by those diplomas and the knowledge and qualifications required by the national rules.

The approach taken by the Court largely resembles what had been agreed upon in Directive 89/48 on the mutual recognition of higher education diplomas. This directive provided for a 'general system for the recognition of higher-education diplomas awarded on completion of professional education and training of at least three years' duration'. It required a general **'mutual recognition'** approach ($\rightarrow$ *7.5*) from which Member States may deviate only in justified situations by requiring either an adaptation period or an aptitude test. This and similar directives have now been replaced by Directive 2005/36 on the recognition of professional qualifications.

In Case C-55/94 *Gebhard* v. *Consiglio dell'ordine degli avvocati e procuratori di Milano* [1995] ECR I-4165, the ECJ most explicitly extended its broad approach against **non-discriminatory rules** developed in the free movement of goods context to the freedom of establishment. The case involved a German lawyer against whom disciplinary measures were taken because he practised law in Italy, although he was not admitted to the Milan Bar and his professional qualifications were not recognised in Italy. The ECJ considered that:

> national measures liable to hinder or make less attractive the exercise of fundamental freedoms guaranteed by the Treaty must fulfil four conditions: they must be applied in a non-discriminatory manner; they must be justified by imperative requirements in the general interest; they must be suitable for securing the attainment of the objective which they pursue; and they must not go beyond what is necessary in order to attain it.

Much of the case law was codified and 'progressively' developed in the so-called **Lawyers' Establishment Directive**. Directive 98/5/EC (to facilitate practise of the profession of lawyer on a permanent basis in a Member State other than that in which the qualification was obtained) now provides that lawyers already admitted in one Member State may immediately practise in another Member State under the professional title acquired in the former state. After effectively and regularly pursuing an activity involving the law of the host Member State for a period of three years, a lawyer will be entitled to admission to the profession and use of the title of that Member State.

8.15 Does the freedom of establishment also apply to companies?

Article 48 TEC provides:

> Companies or firms formed in accordance with the law of
> a Member State and having their registered office, central
> administration or principal place of business within
> the Community shall, for the purposes of this Chapter,
> be treated in the same way as natural persons who are
> nationals of Member States.
>
> 'Companies or firms' means companies or firms
> constituted under civil or commercial law, including
> cooperative societies, and other legal persons governed
> by public or private law, save for those which are non-
> profit-making.

In Case C-212/97 *Centros* v. *Erhvervs- og Selskabsstyrelsen*
[1999] ECR I-1459, the ECJ weakened the position of Member
States wishing to restrict the use of liberal incorporation rules
in other Member States. It held that:

> the fact that a national of a Member State who wishes
> to set up a company chooses to form it in the Member
> State whose rules of company law seem to him the least
> restrictive and to set up branches in other Member
> States cannot, in itself, constitute an abuse of the
> right of establishment. The right to form a company
> in accordance with the law of a Member State and to
> set up branches in other Member States is inherent
> in the exercise, in a single market, of the freedom of
> establishment guaranteed by the Treaty.

Thus, the Danish authorities could not restrict the right of a
company which was incorporated in the UK but did not conduct
any business there to set up a branch in Denmark, even though
they feared that the incorporation in the UK had just been

accomplished in order to circumvent Danish requirements, such as those relating to the payment of a minimum capital for companies. This approach was confirmed by the ECJ in Case C-208/00 *Überseering* v. *NCC* [2002] ECR I-9919, where the Court held that in order to enjoy the rights under Article 43 TEC a company had only to be validly incorporated in one Member State and to have its central administration somewhere in the Community. Thus, German legislation which provided that a company's legal status was governed by the law where it had its central place of administration could not prevent a company incorporated in the Netherlands and having its administrative seat in Germany from operating there, even though it did not comply with all German prudential requirements aimed at protecting the interests of creditors, shareholders and employees.

8.16 What is understood by the freedom to provide services?

While Article 43 permits EC nationals to set up 'permanent' establishments in other Member States ($\rightarrow$ *8.12*), the freedom to **provide services** allows them to operate abroad on a more 'temporal' basis. Article 49(1) TEC provides that:

> Within the framework of the provisions set out below, restrictions on freedom to provide services within the Community shall be prohibited in respect of nationals of Member States who are established in a State of the Community other than that of the person for whom the services are intended.

Although the TEC does not contain a definition of the distinction between establishment and the provision of services, it is clear from the case law of the ECJ that the most important factor is the former's permanent as opposed to the temporary nature of service activities. However, in Case C-55/94 *Gebhard v. Consiglio dell'ordine degli avvocati e procuratori di Milano* [1995] ECR I-4165 (→ *8.14*), the ECJ cautioned that:

> the temporary nature of the activities in question has to be determined in the light, not only of the duration of the provision of the services, but also of its regularity, periodicity or continuity. The fact that the provision of services is temporary does not mean that the provider of services . . . may not equip himself with some form of infrastructure in the host Member State (including an office, chambers or consulting rooms) insofar as such infrastructure is necessary for the purposes of performing the services in question.

8.17 What was the Van Binsbergen Case all about?

In Case 33/74 *Van Binsbergen* v. *Bestuur van de Bedrijsverenigung voor de Metaalnijverheid* [1974] ECR 1299, a Dutch residency requirement for lawyers to be able to provide legal representation services in the Netherlands was ruled to be contrary to Article 49 TEC (→ *8.16*). The ECJ held not only that this article had direct effect, but also that 'the provisions of that article abolish all discrimination against the person providing the service by reason of his nationality or the fact that he is established in a Member State other than that in which the service is to be provided'. With regard to a possible justification of the residency requirement the Court held that:

> The requirement that persons whose functions
> are to assist the administration of justice must be
> permanently established for professional purposes
> within the jurisdiction of certain courts or tribunals

cannot be considered compatible with the provisions
of Article [49 and 50 TEC], where such requirement is
objectively justified by the need to ensure observance of
professional rules of conduct connected, in particular,
with the administration of justice and with respect for
professional ethics.

8.18 Explain the concept of 'passive services'

While Article 49 TEC expressly guarantees the **'provision'** of
services only (→ *8.16*), the ECJ has consistently also held that
persons wishing to **receive services** are **protected** by Community
law. Cases 286/82 and 26/83 *Luisi and Carbone* [1984] ECR 377
involved two Italians who were fined because when travelling
abroad they carried with them foreign currency above the
lawful amount under Italian legislation. They wanted to pay for
services as tourists and recipients of medical treatment. Thus,
the ECJ regarded them as recipients of services and held that
'to go to a State in which the person providing the services is
established' is a **'necessary corollary'** of the freedom to provide
services and thus covered by Article 49 TEC. Thereby the
Court paid tribute to the fact that in some sectors it is usually
the service recipients and not the service providers who have to
travel in order to make the provision of services possible.

This notion of protecting **'service recipients'** was considerably broadened in Case 186/87 *Cowan* v. *Le Trésor Public* [1989]
ECR 195, which concerned a British tourist as a consumer of
services in France. This triggered the application of Article 12
TEC prohibiting discrimination on the basis of nationality. It
was thus held that Cowan, who had been mugged in the Paris
Metro, could not be lawfully excluded from claiming compensation under French crime victim legislation.

? 8.19 What kind of restrictions to the rendering of cross-border services has the ECJ allowed?

Through Article 55 TEC, the **public service** exception as well as **public policy, public security** and **public health** derogations are also relevant for the provision of services (→ *8.9, 8.10*). In addition, the Court has recognised **implicit limitations,** similar to those developed under the *Cassis* **rule of reason** (→ *7.5*).

For instance, in the abovementioned *Van Binsbergen* Case (→ *8.17*) the ECJ, in principle, recognised the need to ensure the **observance of professional** rules, such as 'rules relating to the organization, qualifications, professional ethics, supervision and liability'. In the *German Insurance* Case, Case 205/84 *Commission* v. *Germany* [1986] ECR 3755, the Court acknowledged **consumer protection** considerations as 'imperative reasons relating to the public interest', and in Case C-275/92 *HM Customs and Excise* v. *Schindler* [1994] ECR I-1039, involving the restriction of German lottery ticket sales to the UK, it recognised **social policy grounds.** In Case C-36/02 *Omega* v. *Oberbürgermeisterin der Bundesstadt Bonn* [2004] ECR I-6909, the ECJ acknowledged that the protection of **fundamental rights** was a 'legitimate interest which, in principle, justifies a restriction of the obligations imposed by Community law, even under a fundamental freedom guaranteed by the Treaty such as the freedom to provide services' (→ *6.13, 7.7*).

In a number of cases the Court has made it clear, however, that any **'imperative requirements'** (→ *7.5*) invoked by Member States will be **strictly scrutinised** to ascertain whether they pursue a legitimate aim which is not incompatible with Community law, in a non-discriminatory fashion and in a proportionate manner.

8.20 How did Community legislation facilitate the freedom of establishment and the freedom to provide services?

Initially, the Community pursued a policy of sectoral **harmonisation** through a number of directives providing for minimum standards of professional qualifications in sectors such as the medical profession, nursing, pharmacy, architecture and the legal profession. This piecemeal approach was abandoned by the **Mutual Recognition Directive 89/48** concerning higher education diplomas which introduced a horizontal 'mutual recognition' approach. The basic philosophy of this approach was simple:

(1) it applied to all professions that required a university training of at least three years;
(2) it stated a basic principle of 'mutual recognition' according to which Member States had to recognise professional qualifications acquired in another Member State; and
(3) if the professional training acquired in another Member State differed substantially from the one required in the state where recognition is sought, the latter state was permitted to require either an adaptation period or an aptitude test.

These principles have been carried over to the new **Directive 2005/36** on the **recognition of professional qualifications.**

In 2006, after years of controversy, Directive 2006/123 on services in the internal market was adopted. This so-called **Services Directive** applies to both the 'exercise of the freedom of establishment for service providers and the free movement of services'. It provides for various administrative simplifications to reduce obstacles to the freedom of establishment and services through a 'one-stop-shop' principle in the form of so-called points of single contact. The draft Directive's most controversial idea, that is, that service providers should be regulated by their country of origin and not by the host country, the so-called **country-of-origin principle**, was not kept in the final version. Instead, a rather complex Article 16 now provides that, in principle, the 'Member State in which the service is provided shall ensure free access to and free exercise of a service activity within its territory.' However, in addition to a list of prohibited restrictions, the Directive lays down a number of mandatory requirements that may justify the restriction of the provision of services, such as public policy, public security, public health, the protection of the environment and rules on employment conditions. If Member States stick to these five grounds, the Directive may, indeed, have a liberalising effect. If the ECJ allows them, however, to invoke the further grounds for derogation recognised in its free movement jurisprudence the overall changes will remain modest.

9 EC competition law

In a technical sense, **EC competition policy** covers what is known in many countries as **cartel law** or, as in the United States, 'anti-trust law'. The latter term was adopted because in the late nineteenth century, when anti-trust law was 'invented', most American cartels were established in the form of trusts. EC competition law rests on the triad of a **cartel ban** contained in Article 81 TEC, a **prohibition on market abuse** in Article 82 TEC and **merger control legislation**. All three branches of EC competition law are handled by DG IV, now **DG Competition**, as the Directorate-General for Competition supporting the responsible Commissioner for Competition is known.

In a broader sense, other Community law also contributes to the overall aim of creating conditions for **fair competition within the Common Market**, these include:

(1) treaty provisions on **free movement** as a framework prohibiting mainly public restrictions on the free circulation of goods and services, such as duties and quantitative restrictions and their equivalent counterparts;

(2) special **competition rules** for **public undertakings** in Article 86 TEC; and

(3) the identification and justification or elimination of **subsidies** provided for in the state aid provisions of Articles 87–89 TEC.

? 9.1 What are the economic rationales for the EC's emphasis on competition policy?

As the American debate about the wisdom of anti-trust policies demonstrates, there is still controversy over the need to intervene in the free play of market forces in order to maintain fair competition. The EC pursues a strategy of regulating competition based on the assumption that **effective competition** would **allocate resources** in the **most efficient way, reduce costs** for **consumers, guarantee market access** and openness to new participants and **protect consumers** and **small enterprises against monopolies** ($\rightarrow$ *9.12*). Thus, **competition policy** is regarded as a powerful tool for the creation and preservation of a **single market**. In addition, it complements the EC internal market rules, which aim at the elimination of state imposed tariffs, quotas and measures having equivalent effect, by prohibiting the division of the Common Market by private parties ($\rightarrow$ *7.1*).

? 9.2 Which anti-competitive activities are prohibited by Article 81(1) TEC?

Article 81(1) TEC prohibits:

> as **incompatible** with the common market: all **agreements** between **undertakings, decisions** by associations of undertakings and *concerted practices* which may affect trade between Member States and which have as their object or **effect** the prevention, **restriction or distortion of competition** within the common market.

It continues to list, in a non-exhaustive fashion, **examples of prohibited anti-competitive behaviour**, activities which:

(a) directly or indirectly fix purchase or selling prices or any other trading conditions;

(b) limit or control production, markets, technical development, or investment;

(c) share markets or sources of supply;

(d) apply dissimilar conditions to equivalent transactions with other trading parties, thereby placing them at a competitive disadvantage; and

(e) make the conclusion of contracts subject to acceptance by the other parties of supplementary obligations which, by their nature or according to commercial usage, have no connection with the subject of such contracts.

Article 81(1) TEC is a very broad **prohibition** covering **classic cartels** through price fixing or market sharing. Its concept of restrictive agreements extends to **informal agreements**, not only on a **horizontal** level (between firms on the same production stage) but also in a **vertical** sense (covering, for example, agreements between producers and distributors or the latter and retailers) ($\rightarrow$ *9.5*). As to the notion of an **'agreement'** between undertakings, the Commission and the ECJ have adopted an expansive view, including **oral, non-binding, gentlemen's agreements** as can be seen in the *Quinine Cartel* Case, Cases 41, 44 and 45/69 *ACF Chemiefarma NV* v. *Commission* [1970] ECR 661 and in the *Polypropylene* Case, Commission Decision 86/398 [1986] OJ L230/1.

In a number of cases involving vertical agreements, such as Case C-338/00P *Volkswagen AG* v. *Commission* [2003] ECR I-9189, the Commission and the Community courts have broadly read an 'agreement' into even the unilateral actions of manufacturers trying to dissuade their distributors from exporting goods in order to prevent parallel imports.

More recently, however, in the *Bayer* Case, the ECJ adhered to a narrower notion of agreement. In Joined Cases C-2/01P and C-3/01P *Bundesverband der Arzneimittel-Importeure eV and Commission* v. *Bayer* [2004] ECR I-23, the Court held that:

> for an agreement within the meaning of [Article 81(1)] of the Treaty to be capable of being regarded as having been concluded by tacit acceptance, it is necessary that the manifestation of the wish of one of the contracting parties to achieve an anti-competitive goal constitute an invitation to the other party, whether express or implied, to fulfil that goal jointly, and that applies all the more where, as in this case, such an agreement is not at first sight in the interests of the other party, namely the wholesalers.

Thus, the distribution policy of a pharmaceutical firm that limited deliveries to its distributors in low-price Member States in order to prevent harmful parallel imports into high-price Member States by third parties was regarded as 'only the expression of a unilateral policy of one of the contracting parties', which did not form part of the distribution agreement.

'Decisions by associations of undertakings' were involved in the 1980 *FEDETAB* Case, Joined Cases 209–215 and 218/78 *van Landewyck SARL* v. *Commission* [1980] ECR 3125, where FEDETAB, a Belgian trade association of tobacco manufacturers, promulgated 'recommendations' restricting tobacco distribution. FEDETAB sought an Article 81(3) TEC individual exemption, claiming consumer benefits through upholding choice and other advantages. The ECJ, however, had doubts about these benefits and rejected the claim, because the 'recommendations' eliminated competition in respect of a substantial part of the products in question since FEDETAB members produced or imported 95% of the products in question.

9.3 What are 'concerted practices'?

The most elusive concept contained in Article 81(1) TEC is that of 'concerted practices'. In the so-called *Dyestuffs* Case, Case

48/69 *Imperial Chemical Industries Ltd* v. *Commission* [1972] ECR 619 (→*9.9*), the Court developed a general definition which remains pertinent today. In that case the Commission had fined seventeen dyestuffs producers after three general and uniform price increases between 1964 and 1967. In challenge proceedings before the ECJ, the Court defined 'concerted practices' as:

> a form of **coordination** between undertakings which, without having reached the stage where an agreement properly so-called has been concluded, **knowingly substitutes** practical **cooperation** between them **for** the risks of **competition**.

It continued to regard **parallel behaviour** as strong **evidence**, although insufficient proof in itself, of 'concerted practices'.

This evaluation of parallel behaviour was crucial for the ECJ's partial annulment of a Commission decision in the so-called *Wood Pulp* Case, Joined Cases 89, 104, 114, 116–17 and 125–9/85 *Ahlström Oy* v. *Commission* [1993] ECR I-1307 (→*9.9*). Therein the Court held that:

> parallel conduct cannot be regarded as furnishing proof of concertation unless concertation constitutes the only plausible explanation for such conduct. It is necessary to bear in mind that, although [Article 81] of the Treaty prohibits any form of collusion which distorts competition, it does not deprive economic operators of the right to adapt themselves intelligently to the existing and anticipated conduct of their competitors.

? 9.4 What are the legal consequences of a violation of Article 81(1) TEC?

Where, as a result of an investigation, the Commission finds that an agreement is in violation of Article 81(1) TEC, it is empowered to **impose fines** of up to 10% of an infringing undertaking's turnover. In its fining policy the Commission has to take into account the gravity and duration of the infringement. Since the mid-1990s the Commission has adopted a leniency policy according to which firms cooperating with the Commission's investigations may receive up to 50% reductions in their fines, while so-called 'whistle-blowers' who inform the Commission about the existence of a cartel may even receive total enforcement 'immunity'.

In addition to giving rise to substantial fines, agreements contrary to Article 81(1) TEC are automatically **void** and, thus, unenforceable under Article 81(2) TEC. According to the case law of the ECJ, Article 81(1) TEC infringements may also lead to **liability** in damages for competitors. In Case C-453/99 *Courage* v. *Crehan* [2001] ECR I-6297, the Court again boosted the *effet utile* of Community law by allowing a damages claim for loss caused by anti-competitive contracts or conduct, which may even be raised by a party to the restrictive agreement. According to the Court:

> the existence of such a right strengthens the working of the Community competition rules and discourages agreements or practices, which are frequently covert, which are liable to restrict or distort competition.

9.5 What was the anti-competitive behaviour challenged in Consten and Grundig?

Joined Cases 56 and 58/64 *Établissements Consten S.à.R.L. and Grundig-Verkaufs-GmbH* v. *Commission* [1966] ECR 299, is one of the early leading competition law cases, evidencing that Article 81(1) TEC does not prohibit only the classical 'horizontal' cartels but also certain **'vertical' agreements** ($\rightarrow$ *9.2*). It involved a German electronics producer, Grundig, who appointed Consten as sole distributor in France enabling it to exclude Grundig products put on the market in other Member States. For this purpose, Grundig assigned to Consten its French trademark, GINT, in order to exclude parallel imports. When a French competitor of Consten started to import from Germany, which was substantially cheaper, he was sued by Consten for trademark infringement and unfair competition resulting from knowingly violating its contractual terms with Grundig. In this law-suit the French competitor argued that the contract between Grundig and Consten was invalid because it contravened Article 81(1) TEC (→ 9.4).

At the same time, the Commission denied Consten's request for an exemption under Article 81(3) TEC (→ 9.12), citing the substantially higher prices for Grundig products on the French market. In the ensuing annulment action, the ECJ upheld the Commission's decision and found a violation of Article 81(1) TEC in the absolute territorial protection and the GINT assignment, not, however, in the exclusive dealing provisions which were severable and remained legally binding. In effect, the Court affirmed the concept of a 'vertical restraint' which led to an isolation of the French market:

> Competition may be distorted within the meaning of Article [81(1)] of the EEC Treaty not only by agreements which limit it as between the parties but also by agreements which prevent or restrict the competition which might take place between one of them and third parties. For this purpose it is irrelevant whether the parties to the agreement are or are not on a footing of equality as regards their position and function in the economy.
>
> A sole distributorship contract may, without involving an abuse of a dominant position, affect trade between the Member States and at the same time have as its object or effect the prevention, restriction or distortion of competition, thus falling under the prohibition of Article [81(1)] of the EEC Treaty.

? 9.6 Why can the determination of what constitutes an 'undertaking' in the sense of Article 81 TEC be of crucial importance in competition cases?

The Treaty does not define the term 'undertaking'. However, the Commission and the European courts have broadly understood 'undertakings' to include **any entity** engaged in an **economic/commercial activity** regardless of its legal status and financing, a definition that comprises trade associations, partnerships, individuals, and state-owned corporations as long as they do not exercise public law powers. For the latter reason, the Court found in the *Eurocontrol* Case, Case C-364/92 *SAT Fluggesellschaft* v. *Eurocontrol* [1994] ECR I-43, that international organisations may escape the qualification as an 'undertaking'. It held that Eurocontrol's activities:

> by their nature, their aim and the rules to which they
> are subject, are connected with the exercise of powers
> relating to the control and supervision of air space which
> are typically those of a public authority. They are not
> of an economic nature justifying the application of the
> Treaty rules of competition.

According to the **'single enterprise doctrine'**, which was aptly captured by the ECJ in Case 15/74 *Centrafarm BV et Adriaan de Peijper* v. *Sterling Drug Inc.* [1974] ECR 1147, agreements between legally distinct firms may not fall under the cartel prohibition of Article 81(1) TEC if they 'form an **economic unit** within which the **subsidiary** has **no real freedom** to determine its course of action on the market'. Similarly, the Court concluded in the *Dyestuffs* Case (→ *9.3*) that:

> where a subsidiary does not enjoy real autonomy on
> determining its course of action in the market, the
> prohibitions set out in [Article 81(1) TEC] may be
> considered inapplicable in the relationship between it and

the parent company with which it forms one economic unit.

One should be aware, however, that the inapplicability of Article 81 TEC may open up the possibility of using Article 82 TEC if the single enterprise is found to be in a **dominant position** (→ *9.17*) which it abuses, as the ECJ reminded us in the so-called *Parker Pen* Case, Case C-73/95P *Viho Europe* v. *Commission* [1996] ECR I-5457, where a producer bought all its formerly independent distributors and, thus, avoided scrutiny of its distribution practices under Article 81 TEC.

? 9.7 When does anti-competitive behaviour 'affect trade between Member States'?

The ECJ held in *Consten and Grundig* (→ *9.5*) that restrictive behaviour may reach Community relevance if it is 'capable of constituting a threat, either direct or indirect, actual or potential, to freedom of trade between Member States in a manner which might harm the attainment of the objectives of a single market between States'; a test closely resembling the *Dassonville* formula, laid down in the leading case on the free movement of goods, Case 8/74 *Procureur du Roi* v. *Dassonville* [1974] ECR 837 (→ *7.3*).

Thus, purely national cartels fall outside the scope of Article 81(1) TEC. However, in practice the Court is likely to liberally accept a Community effect. In Case 8/72 *Cementhandelaren* v. *Commission* [1972] ECR 977, the ECJ found a Common Market effect with the following reasoning:

> An agreement extending over the whole of the territory
> of a Member State by its very nature has the effect
> of reinforcing the compartmentalization of markets
> on a national basis, thereby holding up the economic

interpenetration which the Treaty is designed to bring about and protecting national production.

However, according to the Court's *de minimis* rule, as explained in Case 5/69 *Völk* v. *Vervaecke* [1969] ECR 295, an effect on inter-state trade that is not noticeable 'may escape the prohibition laid down in [Article 81(1) TEC]'.

? 9.8 How has the Commission acted in order to clarify the Court's *de minimis* rule?

The judge-made *de minimis* rule has been clarified in a series of Commission Notices since 1970. The 1986 Commission Notice on Agreements of Minor Importance excluded Commission review if an agreement represented less than 5% of the market share and if the aggregate annual turnover did not exceed 300 million ECUs, the predecessor currency to the Euro. These thresholds have been repeatedly amended and currently provide for a 5% combined market share of participating undertakings in cases of vertical agreements, 10% in cases of horizontal agreements between competitors and 15% in cases of non-competitors. They are laid down in the 2001 Commission Notice on Agreements of Minor Importance which do not Appreciably Restrict Competition under Article 81(1) (*de minimis*), OJ 2001 C 368/13.

Things are further complicated by the Commission Guidelines on the Effect on Trade Concept contained in Articles 81 and 82 of the Treaty, OJ 2004 C 101/81, according to which agreements are considered outside the scope of Community law if the parties' aggregate market share is less than 5% and if, in cases of horizontal agreements, their aggregate turnover does not exceed €40 million or, in cases of vertical agreements, the turnover of the supplier is less than €40 million. It should be kept in mind, however, that if an agreement is considered to be

below the threshold of Community law, it may still be governed
by national competition rules.

? 9.9 Does the Treaty prohibit anti-competitive behaviour abroad that merely produces effects in the Community?

The Commission clearly investigates and fines violations of EC
competition law on an **extraterritorial basis**. So far, the ECJ has
managed to avoid the issue. In the *Dyestuffs* Case (→ *9.3*, *9.6*),
Case 48/69 *Imperial Chemical Industries Ltd* v. *Commission*
[1972] ECR 619, it found that the actions of a UK firm, at a time
before the UK had joined the Community, were **carried on**
directly **within the Community** because, as a result of the 'single
economic unit' doctrine (→ *9.6*), the actions of its European
subsidiary could be attributed to the parent:

> The fact that a subsidiary has separate legal personality
> is not sufficient to exclude the possibility of imputing its
> conduct to the parent company.
>
> Such may be the case in particular where the
> subsidiary, although having separate legal personality,
> does not decide independently upon its own conduct on
> the market, but carries out, in all material respects, the
> instructions given to it by the parent company.

In the later *Wood Pulp* Case, Joined Cases 89, 104, 114, 116–17,
125–9/85 *Ahlström Oy* v. *Commission* [1993] ECR I-1307 (→ *9.3*),
it found that where foreign wood pulp producers sold directly to
purchasers in the EC and engaged in price competition in order
to win orders from those customers, such activity constituted
competition 'within' the Common Market. The ECJ further
distinguished between formation and implementation of agreements and held that the place where they are implemented was
'decisive'.

❓ 9.10 Is the extraterritorial application of EC competition law permissible under public international law?

As a matter of principle, each state, or other entity exercising state-like legislative functions such as the EC in the field of competition law, has the **power to regulate** things and persons situated **within its territory**. This so-called jurisdiction to prescribe may sometimes also extend beyond a state's territory when protecting core state interests, for example, against espionage or the counterfeiting of its currency, under the 'protective principle'. Another enlargement of the territorial principle of jurisdiction to prescribe is the so-called **effects doctrine**, used mainly in international criminal law, according to which a state may regulate behaviour abroad if that behaviour **produces effects** within its territory. The famous gun-shot across a state border is the textbook example.

In international economic law, this **effects principle** seems to be increasingly accepted in the field of **anti-trust/ competition law**. This, of course, makes perfect business sense because otherwise national or EC competition law might be easily avoided by managers simply flying off to a remote place outside the Community in order to fix their restrictive agreements. It remains, however, a conceptual challenge to the prevailing territoriality principle of international law, allocating to states jurisdiction to prescribe along mainly territorial lines.

In 1991 the US and the EC entered into an agreement regarding the application of their competition rules which aimed at avoiding conflicts over enforcement activities resulting from mutual extraterritorial claims. Each party stipulated, in particular, to take into account the relative significance of the conduct and its effect on the other party. It was replaced by a 1998 Agreement between the European Communities and the

Government of the United States of America regarding the application of their competition laws after it had been annulled by the ECJ in Case 327/91 *France* v. *Commission* [1994] ECR I-3641 for formal reasons (→ *11.4*).

? 9.11 Are all economic activities covered by the prohibition of Article 81(1) TEC?

In addition to express exceptions for nuclear energy such as those in Article 305(2) TEC, national security as contained in Article 296 TEC and, to a more limited extent, for services of **general economic interest** under Article 86(2) TEC (→ *9.32*), the ECJ has clarified that **certain agreements** fall **outside** the scope of **EC competition law**.

In Joined Cases C-115/97, C-116/97 and C-117/97 *Brentjens' Handelsonderneming BV* v. *Stichting Bedrijfspensioenfonds voor Handel in Bovwmaterialen* [1999] ECR I-6025, it found that **collective bargaining** agreements are excluded from EC competition law because:

> the social policy objectives pursued by such agreements would be seriously undermined if management and labour were subject to [Article 81(1)] of the Treaty when seeking jointly to adopt measures to improve conditions of work and employment.

In Case C-309/99 *Wouters* v. *Algemene Raad van de Nederlandse Orde van Advocaten* [2002] ECR I-1577, the Court held that a national regulation prohibiting so-called multidisciplinary partnerships between lawyers and accountants 'adopted by a body such as the Bar of the Netherlands does not infringe [Article 81(1)] of the Treaty, since that body could reasonably have considered that that regulation, despite the effects restrictive of competition that are inherent in it, is necessary for the proper practice of the legal profession, as organised in the Member State concerned'. Whether, and to what extent, other Treaty aims and national interests may be held to be generally exempted from EC competition law remains to be seen. What is clear, however, is the fact that Article 81 TEC itself provides for certain exceptions from its prohibition.

9.12 Under what condition may a cartel be exempted from the prohibition of Article 81(1) TEC?

Community law provides for the permissibility of restrictive agreements which may encourage competition in another way. Article 81(3) TEC makes such **exemptions** conditional upon the requirement that the agreement in question:

> contributes to improving the production or distribution of goods or to promoting technical or economic progress, while allowing consumers a fair share of the resulting benefit, and which does not:
>
> (a) impose on the undertakings concerned restrictions which are not indispensable to the attainment of these objectives;
>
> (b) afford such undertaking the possibility of eliminating competition in respect of a substantial part of the products in question.

While in the early days of EC Competition Policy Article 81(3) TEC **exemptions** always had to be granted by the Commission either on an **individual** or on a **general** basis, the reform of EC competition law pursuant to Regulation 1/2003 (→ 9.16) makes Article 81(3) TEC **directly applicable** (→ 4.4) and, thus, leaves the assessment whether an agreement may benefit from the exemption or not to the affected companies themselves and to **national competition authorities**. While economic efficiency is the major consideration in determining whether an agreement 'contributes to improving the production or distribution of goods or to promoting technical or economic progress', the practice of the Community institutions shows that also other Community interests, such as environmental or industrial policy goals, may play a certain role in this assessment.

? 9.13 What is the purpose of 'group exemptions'?

In 1965 the Council authorised the Commission in Regulation 19/65 to formulate group 'declarations of inapplicability' under Article 81(3) TEC. These declarations, also referred to as 'group' or 'block exemptions', eliminate the notification requirement for entire groups of agreements and, thus, reduce the administrative burden for the Commission. These regulations typically include a 'black list' of prohibited restrictions and a 'white list' of permissible provisions. Agreements falling under such 'group' or 'block exemptions' do not need to be notified to the Commission; they are instead exempted automatically.

The economic justification for exempting certain agreements from the cartel prohibition of Article 81(1) TEC is not always free from controversy (→ 9.1). With regard to exclusive distribution agreements, for example, it has been argued that they facilitate costly market access to newcomers and thereby foster the idea of the Common Market. They are further considered to be beneficial because the exclusive retailers will add marketing efforts to sell a manufacturer's brand and, thus, increase so-called inter-brand competition. At the same time, the exclusive distribution agreement will discourage customers from seeking pre-sales services from exclusive retailers and then buying from cheaper competitors. This elimination of so-called intra-brand competition prevents free-riders from benefiting from the exclusive retailers' increased marketing efforts.

On the other hand, exclusive distribution agreements with territorial protection may disintegrate the Common Market – as was recognised in the 1966 *Consten and Grundig* Case (→ *9.5*). Sometimes pre-sales services may be unwanted by consumers and merely increase the price of the products they are seeking. Additionally, exclusive distribution agreements may prevent competing manufacturers from entering a market.

9.14 Which kind of Community legislation is used to grant 'group exemptions'?

Contrary to individual exemptions, which were granted in the form of decisions, the Commission enacts 'group exemptions' in the form of regulations. Since the first block exemption, Regulation 67/67 on exclusive purchasing agreements, such exemptions have been laid down in a series of Community regulations, exempting among others certain research and development agreements (Regulation 2659/00), specialisation agreements (Regulation 2658/00) and technology transfer (Regulation 240/96) among others.

The block exemptions system had the advantage of avoiding the slow individual exemption route. However, since it basically required parties to structure their agreements according to the permissible clauses contained in the various block exemption regulations it was increasingly criticised as being too formalistic and narrow and providing a strait-jacket for business partners. Thus, by the mid-1990s the Commission revised its competition policy on vertical restraints. The regulations concerning exclusive distribution agreements (Regulation 1983/83), exclusive purchasing agreements (Regulation 1984/83) and franchise agreements (Regulation 4087/88) expired by the end of 1999 and were replaced by the so-called Vertical Restraints Block Exemption Regulation 2790/1999. This regulation entered into force on 1 June 2000 and covers most vertical agreements involving the sale of goods or services. It renders the prohibition of Article 81(1) TEC inapplicable to vertical agreements entered into by companies with market shares not exceeding 30%. Further, Regulation 2790/1999 still contains a 'black list' of prohibited clauses, such as price fixing or most territorial protection clauses. It also prohibits a number of non-compete obligations aimed at preventing access to a distribution network by competitors. In response to the charge of having been too legalistic in the past, the Commission noted in its Guidelines on Vertical Restraints, OJ 2000 C291/1, that it will adopt an 'economic approach' in the application of Article 81 TEC to vertical restraints.

9.15 Outline the basic procedure under Regulation 17

For a long time, Regulation 17/62, adopted by the Council in 1962, provided the procedural framework for the enforcement of European Competition Law by the Commission. It rested on broad notification requirements imposed on companies, complaints by competitors and sweeping investigation powers given to the Commission.

According to the Regulation, agreements contrary to Article 81(1) TEC had to be notified to the Commission. The Commission then had a number of options from which to choose: it could issue a so-called comfort letter, an informal statement asserting that it saw no reason to intervene in opposition to the activities notified; it could give a 'negative clearance' certifying that 'on the basis of the facts in its possession, there are no grounds . . . for action'; or it could grant individual exemptions to the parties by declaring Article 81(1) TEC inapplicable according to Article 81(3) TEC (→ 9.12).

Individual exemptions thus granted by the Commission were open to **modification** by subsequent Commission decisions in case of:

(1) a change in any of the facts which were basic to the making of the decision;
(2) a breach of any obligation attached to the decision;
(3) a decision was based on incorrect information or was induced by deceit; or
(4) an abuse of the exemption.

If the Commission concluded that the notified agreement **contravened** Article 81(1) TEC, it would have the power to **prohibit** it and **impose fines** on the offending firms.

For all Commission competition decisions, **judicial review** was available through the ECJ. Since 1989 such challenges first go to the CFI and can reach the ECJ on appeal ($\rightarrow$ *5.3, 5.6*). In the past, the European courts have repeatedly reduced the fines imposed by the Commission. For instance, in the *Cement Cartel* Case, Joined Cases T-25/95 *Cimenteries CBR SA and others* v. *Commission* [2000] ECR II-491, the CFI reduced the total fine of approximately €250 million to around €110 million.

? 9.16   Outline the reform of EC competition law enforcement

In December 2002, the Council adopted **Regulation 1/2003** on the implementation of the rules on competition laid down in Articles 81 and 82 of the Treaty. With its entry into force in May 2004, this regulation replaced Regulation 17/62. It embodies a radical reform by **decentralising** and **simplifying** the existing **competition law procedure**. The new regulation abolishes the Commission's power to grant individual exemptions. Instead, business firms have to ensure that their agreements do not violate Article 81(1) TEC or, in case they do, that the restrictive practices qualify under Article 81(3) TEC (→ *9.12*). There is thus greater reliance on **block exemptions**. At the same time, the Commission is partly replaced by **national competition authorities**. This became legally feasible by making the provisions of Article 81(3) TEC directly applicable (→*4.4, 9.12*), thus, allowing enforcement of the rules governing restrictive practices by national competition authorities and national courts. By 2002 the Commission and the national competition authorities had already created a network of competition authorities, the 'European Competition Network', which provides for the allocation of cases according to the principle of the best-placed authority and ensures investigation cooperation between its members.

There are a number of safeguards in the new regulation to ensure cooperation, while at the same time providing an ultimate 'watchdog' role for the Commission. Regulation 1/2003 provides, for instance, that the Commission be consulted before decisions applying Articles 81 or 82 TEC are taken. Moreover, there are rules on suspending parallel national proceedings once the Commission or a national competition authority have commenced **investigations** in a particular case. Finally, the Commission has the opportunity to continue to deal with cases affecting more than three Member States, and the Commission's investigatory powers have been broadened. Under the control of national judges, its search rights also extend to private homes of business executives if there is a reasonable suspicion that business records, which may be relevant to prove a serious violation of Article 81 or Article 82 TEC, are kept there.

9.17 How does EC competition law regulate dominant market power?

The second main pillar of EC competition law is the prohibition of **abuse** of a **dominant market** position found in Article 82 TEC. It provides as follows:

> Any **abuse** by one or more undertakings of a **dominant position** within the common market or in a substantial part of it shall be **prohibited** as incompatible with the common market in so far as it may affect trade between Member States.
>
> Such abuse may, in particular, consist in:
>
> (a) directly or indirectly imposing unfair purchase or selling prices or other unfair trading conditions;
> (b) limiting production, markets or technical development to the prejudice of consumers;
> (c) applying dissimilar conditions to equivalent transactions with other trading parties, thereby placing them at a competitive disadvantage; and
> (d) making the conclusion of contracts subject to acceptance by the other parties of supplementary obligations which, by their nature or according to commercial usage, have no connection with the subject of such contracts.

9.18 When does an undertaking enjoy a 'dominant position'?

Article 82 TEC is very clear in **not** making **monopoly** (or oligopoly) power **illegal** *per se*. Instead, it requires an **abuse** of a dominant position which may also be held collectively. On the other hand, otherwise abusive practices under Article 82 TEC may not be prohibited if engaged in by a firm lacking market dominance.

Thus, for any analysis under Article 82 TEC, it is crucial to determine the existence of **market dominance**, which remains undefined in the Treaty. In Case 27/76 *United Brands* v. *Commission* [1978] ECR 207, the ECJ defined this concept as:

> a position of **economic strength** enjoyed by an undertaking which enables it to **prevent** effective **competition** being maintained on the relevant market by giving it the power to **behave** to an appreciable extent **independently** of its competitors, its customers and ultimately of the consumers.

In practice, the Commission has prosecuted in instances where market share is 40%, such as in the *United Brands* Case (→ *9.19, 9.23*). However, even a market share of more than 40% may not be sufficient for a finding of dominance in the absence of other factors, as the Court held in Case 85/76 *Hoffmann-La Roche* v. *Commission* [1979] ECR 461. According to the *Michelin* Case, Case 322/81 *Nederlandse Banden-Industrie Michelin NV* v. *Commission* [1983] ECR 3461, it depends upon the 'relative economic strength' of a company, which means that dominance will depend upon the **market shares** of the **competitors**, and, as the Court has held in the *United Brands* Case, even a low market share may imply dominance if there are significant entry barriers to (potential) competitors.

? 9.19 What is the relevant market in order to determine a dominant position?

Market dominance is not only an economic concept, sometimes difficult for lawyers to grasp, it is also a relative concept relating to: (1) a **product market** and (2) a **geographical market** and comprising (3) a **temporal factor**.

Legal battles have been fought over the scope of the relevant product market which may be decisive for a finding of dominance and, thus, the applicability of Article 82 TEC. The Commission and the Court have focused on the **interchangeability** of products. From a demand side, this requires that high **cross-elasticity** be shown, that is, the willingness of buyers to substitute product B for product A if the price of product A has been raised. There may be other factors in determining a product market, such as a product's **objective physical characteristics**. Obviously, it is sometimes not so easy to make a choice. The ECJ's reasoning in the abovementioned *United Brands* Case (→ *9.18*, *9.23*) offers some of the most entertaining reading in EC jurisprudence. In finding that the banana market was sufficiently distinct from the other fresh fruit market, the Court made the following remarks:

> The banana has certain characteristics, appearance,
> taste, softness, seedlessness, easy handling, a constant
> level of production which enable it to satisfy the
> constant needs of an important section of the population
> consisting of the very young, the old and the sick . . .
> It follows from all these considerations that a very
> large number of consumers having a constant need for
> bananas are not noticeably or even appreciably enticed
> away from the consumption of this product by the arrival
> of fresh fruit on the market and that even the seasonal
> peak periods only affect it for a limited period of time
> from the point of view of substitutability.

From a supply-side perspective products will be considered interchangeable if they can be produced by a simple change in the production process, as was demonstrated in the *Continental Can* Case (→ *9.20*).

? 9.20 Why is the Continental Can Case so important to EC competition law?

Case 6-72 *Europemballage Corporation and Continental Can Company Inc.* v. *Commission* [1973] ECR 215, is another leading case on **market definition**. The Court annulled a Commission decision differentiating between separate markets for preserved meat, shellfish cans and metal tops which did not state the difference in markets for containers of other goods (for example, fruit and vegetables). The ECJ focused on **interchangeability** from a supply-side and held that:

> In order to be regarded as constituting a distinct market, the products in question must be individualized, not only by the mere fact that they are used for packaging certain products, but by particular characteristics of production which make them specifically suitable for that purpose. Consequently, a dominant position on the market for light metal containers for meat and fish cannot be decisive, as long as it has not been proved that competitors from other sectors of the market for light metal containers are not in a position to enter this market, by a simple adaptation, with sufficient strength to create a serious counterweight.

The *Continental Can* Case was also important for the Community's **merger control** before the 1989 Merger Regulation was adopted (→ *9.26–30*). The Commission found an abuse of a dominant position in Continental Can's acquisition of a Dutch metal can producer after having already acquired a dominant position on the relevant market by acquiring 85% in a German metal can producer.

9.21 Which other factors are important for market definition?

While the relevant **geographical market** may in some cases be the entire Common Market, technical and practical obstacles in product distribution may require a narrower concept of the relevant market. It may be the territory of a single Member

State or even parts of it, as long as the objective conditions of competition applying to certain products are identical for all traders.

Equally, a **temporal element** may be important, since certain product markets may be seasonally determined or even more generally subject to change due to technological progress and shifting consumer preferences.

In order to make the arcane subject of market definition somewhat more transparent and accessible, the **Commission** published a **Notice** on the **Definition of the Relevant Market** for the Purposes of Community Competition Law, OJ 1997 C372/5, which primarily follows a demand-side substitutability test. According to the Commission:

> the question to be answered is whether the parties' customers would switch to readily available substitutes or to suppliers located elsewhere in response to a hypothetical small (in the range of 5 to 10%) but permanent relative price increase in the products and areas being considered. If substitution were enough to make the price increase unprofitable because of the resulting loss of sales, additional substitutes and areas are included in the relevant market. This would be done until the set of products and geographical areas is such that small, permanent increases in relative prices would be profitable.

9.22 What kind of behaviour amounts to an 'abuse' in the sense of Article 82 TEC?

Article 82 TEC itself provides a number of examples of an **abuse**, such as imposing unfair prices and trading conditions, limiting production, applying dissimilar conditions to equivalent transactions (discriminatory pricing, etc.) and subjecting contracts to unconnected supplementary obligations (tying). However, the precise scope of abusive practices made illegal by the Treaty is difficult to ascertain and has been refined by the practice of the Commission and the European courts. While most of the examples listed in the non-exhaustive enumeration of Article 82 TEC (→ 9.17) are forms of so-called exploitative abuse, primarily harming consumers as a result of unrivalled monopoly or quasi-monopoly power, European competition law practice has equally used Article 82 TEC in order to fight so-called exclusionary abuse whereby dominant firms try to eliminate competitors from the market (→ 9.1).

? 9.23 Which were the abusive practices of United Brands?

In addition to its importance with regard to market definition (→ 9.19), Case 27/76 *United Brands* v. *Commission* [1978] ECR 207, is one of the leading competition law cases concerning **abusive behaviour**. It involved the largest banana producing firm which owned, among others, the brand 'Chiquita'. The trade restrictive activities, for which United Brands was fined by the Commission, comprise a text-book sample of abusive practices:

(a) **Unfair pricing** According to the Commission, the difference between actual costs and price was excessive. This point was, however, rejected by the Court since it was not adequately proven by the Commission. The Court accepted that the sales in Ireland might have been made at loss to gain market access.

(b) **Refusal to deal** United Brands refused to supply a Danish distributor with Chiquita bananas because he had also become the sole distributor of competing 'Dole' bananas. The ECJ regarded such behaviour as inconsistent with

Article 82(b) and (c) TEC 'since the refusal to sell would limit markets to the prejudice of consumers and would amount to discrimination which might in the end eliminate a trading party from the relevant market.'

(c) **Discriminatory pricing** United Brands charged its Irish distributors 50% less than its Danish one. In a not wholly uncontroversial ruling, the ECJ upheld the Commission's finding of abusive price discrimination, obviously inspired by the goal of creating a single market: 'a rigid partitioning of national markets was thus created at price levels which were artificially different, placing certain distributors/ ripeners at a comparative disadvantage, since compared with what it should have been competition had thereby been distorted'.

9.24 What is the 'essential facilities doctrine'?

As in *United Brands*, the ECJ found an abuse of a dominant position in a **refusal to supply** a customer in the *Commercial Solvents* Case, Joined Cases 6 and 7/73 *Istituto Chemioterapico Italiano SpA* v. *Commission* [1974] ECR 233. It was a special aspect of this case that the customer had also become a competitor of the dominant firm as a result of the latter's decision to move into the production of pharmaceuticals originally only made by the customer. What was important in this case was the fact that the raw materials that were subject to the refusal to supply were 'essential' to the customer's production.

Based on such cases, the Commission developed a practice according to which refusal to grant **access** to an 'essential facility' may constitute **abuse**. In particular, the transport and telecommunications sector was targeted by the Commission. The problem lies in defining the scope of such a facility, because it basically refers to something owned or controlled by a dominant firm to which others need access in order to provide products or services to their customers. In Case C-7/97 *Oscar Bronner* v. *Mediaprint* [1998] ECR I-7791, the ECJ held that a newspaper home delivery service maintained by a dominant publisher did not constitute an 'essential' facility for the distribution of newspapers to which a competing publisher with a small market share would have to be granted access. According to the ECJ's very restrictive standard in *Bronner*, the dominant firm's refusal to supply its delivery service to a competitor would be abusive only if it were likely to eliminate the competitor from the market, if access was 'indispensable', if there was no available alternative and if there was no objective justification for refusing to cooperate. In addition, one should not overlook the fact that the *Bronner* Case concerned a situation where a dominant firm refused to establish commercial relations with a competitor, whereas a case like *Commercial Solvents* concerned a refusal to continue such relations.

In the *Microsoft* Case, Case COMP/C 3/37.792 *Microsoft-Antitrust* [2004] EC Comm. 1, however, the Commission reverted to the 'essential facilities' doctrine and found that Microsoft had abused its dominant position by not disclosing 'inter-operability information' which would have allowed competitors to design competing products in the 'work groups server' market. Microsoft's challenge of the Commission decision before the CFI in Case T-201/04 *Microsoft* v. *Commission* [2007] ECR II-3601, was largely unsuccessful.

9.25 What is 'predatory pricing'?

'Predatory pricing' is the internal equivalent to what would constitute 'dumping' in the context of external trade ($\rightarrow$

11.2). The leading case is Case C-62/86 *AKZO Chemie* v. *Commission* [1991] ECR I-3359, in which a dominant firm targeted the customers of its competitor, offering them extremely low prices (below cost) in order to eliminate the competitor. Such elimination may result even if the competitor is just as efficient as the dominant firm but lacks comparable financial resources to sustain the 'price war'. Below-cost sales are often financed through a form of cross-subsidisation as in Case C-333/94P *Tetra-Pak* v. *Commission* [1996] ECR I-5951. Tetra-Pak had a dominant position in the market for aseptic packaging cartons for food and used its profits made there in order to subsidise its below-cost sales of non-aseptic cartons. According to the CFI in Case T-228/97 *Irish Sugar plc* v. *Commission* [1999] ECR II-2969, a dominant firm may, however, justify its aggressive pricing policy if it is intended to protect its market position, is based on efficiency and is in the interests of the consumers.

9.26 Are mergers and acquisitions prohibited by the EC Treaty?

The issue of mergers is not expressly mentioned in the TEC and, while, for a long time, Member States were unable to agree on secondary legislation to fill this gap, the European competition law enforcers and the ECJ helped out by applying the existing competition rules contained in Articles 81 and 82 TEC in a broad fashion.

It clearly was a matter of contention in Case 6/72 *Europemballage Corporation and Continental Can Company Inc.* v. *Commission* [1973] ECR 215, when the Commission objected to a control bid for a Dutch competitor by Continental Can, a firm which already enjoyed a dominant position in the market (→ *9.20*). The ECJ upheld this decision stating that:

> abuse may therefore occur if an undertaking in a
> dominant position strengthens such position in such a way
> that the degree of dominance reached substantially fetters
> competition, i.e. that only undertakings remain in the
> market whose behaviour depends on the dominant one.

In 1987 the ECJ held in the *Philip Morris* Case, Joined Cases 142 and 156/84 *British American Tobacco Co. Ltd and R. J. Reynolds Industries Inc.* v. *Commission* [1987] ECR 4487, that Article 81 TEC could also apply to the acquisition of shares in a competitor if that acquisition could influence the behaviour in the marketplace of the companies involved.

9.27 Describe the main features of the Commission's merger control

In December 1989, the time was finally ripe for **Community legislation** in the field of **mergers**, which are referred to as 'concentrations' in Community law. Council Regulation 4064/89 on the Control of Concentrations between Undertakings, as amended by Regulation 1310/97 and now embodied in Regulation 139/2004, empowers the **Merger Task Force** of the Commission to **oppose** large-scale (Community relevant) **mergers and acquisitions**. It sets out the following procedure:

(1) Intended concentrations must be **notified** to the Commission within one week after the agreement to merge, announcement of a takeover bid, or the like. Any proposed merger is on hold while being investigated by the Commission.

(2) A substantive **Common Market compatibility check** is carried out by the Commission in two stages: first, it decides within one month whether a proposed concentration falls under the Regulation, whether it is compatible with the

Common Market or, if there are serious doubts about that, whether an investigation should be initiated. Second, the Common Market compatibility will be investigated during a period usually not exceeding four months.

Commission decisions blocking or conditioning mergers upon the fulfilment of burdensome prerequisites are subject to judicial review (→ *5.3, 5.6*). The European courts have adopted a strict scrutiny standard for merger cases. As explained in Case C-12/03 *Commission* v. *Tetra-Laval* [2005] ECR I-987, they will not only 'establish whether the evidence relied on is factually accurate, reliable and consistent but also whether that evidence contains all the information which must be taken into account in order to assess a complex situation and whether it is capable of substantiating the conclusions drawn from it'. Thus, where, in Case T-310/01 *Schneider Electric SA* v. *Commission* [2002] ECR II-4071, for example, they found 'errors, omissions and inconsistencies . . . in the Commission's analysis of undoubted gravity' they annulled Commission decisions to block mergers.

? 9.28 What are 'concentrations'?

The Community term for mergers and acquisitions is 'concentrations'. According to the Merger Regulation, any kind of acquiring control over a firm, for example, a merger agreement, a stock or asset purchase, may qualify as concentration. A particular problem is posed by various forms of so-called joint ventures which cover all kinds of arrangements between firms, from loose cooperation, to strategic alliances, to strict integration. It is fairly obvious that only 'concentrative' joint ventures are subject to the Merger Regulation, while 'cooperative' joint ventures remain subject to Article 81 TEC. The real problem lies in distinguishing between the two forms in practice. According to Article 3(2) of the Merger Regulation, 'the creation of a joint venture performing on a lasting basis all the functions of an autonomous economic entity shall constitute a concentration . . .' The Commission has shed some further light on this concept in its Notice on Full Function Joint Ventures, OJ 1998 C66/1.

9.29 How does EC law ensure that only Community relevant mergers and acquisitions are regulated by the Merger Regulation?

The Merger Regulation contains quantitative Community thresholds triggering its application. According to the one-stop shop principle, once the Merger Regulation applies there is no need to seek approval from national authorities in the Member States. According to Article 1(2) of the Merger Regulation a concentration has a 'Community dimension' if: (a) the combined world-wide turnover of all affected undertakings exceeds €5 billion; and (b) the Community-wide turnover of each of at least two affected undertakings exceeds €250 million, unless each of the undertakings achieves more than two-thirds of its aggregate Community-wide turnover within one and the same Member State. This rule is supplemented by alternative (lower) thresholds for companies operating in more than two Member States.

In addition there are rules providing for some flexibility as regards the question of who should investigate mergers and acquisitions:

> According to the so-called 'German clause' in Article 9 of the Merger Regulation, the Commission may refer a Community relevant merger to national authorities, if a distinct market exists within the Member State and the concentration 'threatens to create or strengthen a dominant

position [therein] as a result of which effective competition would be significantly impeded'. In practice, the number of referrals to national competition authorities under this clause has been low.

Pursuant to the 'Dutch clause' (the Netherlands, like Belgium and Italy, did not have merger control legislation in the early 1990s) of Article 22 of the Merger Regulation, the Commission may enforce the Merger Regulation even below the relevant thresholds at a Member State's request.

Article 21 of the Merger Regulation also mentions certain 'legitimate interests' of Member States, such as 'public security, plurality of the media and prudential rules', as possible reasons to exempt certain concentrations from its merger rules.

9.30 Under what conditions may 'concentrations' be approved?

Under Article 2(1) of the Merger Regulation the Commission will take into account the following criteria in order to assess the Common Market compatibility of a proposed merger:

(a) the need to maintain and develop effective competition within the Common Market in view of, among other things, the structure of all the markets concerned and the actual or potential competition from undertakings located either within or outwith the Community;

(b) the market position of the undertakings concerned and their economic and financial power, the alternatives available to suppliers and users, their access to suppliers or markets, any legal or other barriers to entry, supply and demand trends for the relevant goods and services, the interests of the intermediate and ultimate consumers and the development of technical and economic progress provided that it is to consumers' advantage and does not form an obstacle to competition.

In its Guidelines on the Assessment of Horizontal Mergers under the Council Regulation on the Control of Concentrations between Undertakings, OJ 2004 C31/5, the Commission has specified the methods it intends to use in order to scrutinise a proposed merger's Common Market compatibility.

If, on the basis of such an assessment, the **Commission** concludes that a proposed concentration would 'create or strengthen a dominant position as a result of which effective competition would be significantly impeded in the Common Market', Article 2(3) of the Merger Regulation provides that it has the power to **declare** it **incompatible** with the Common Market. Out of the approximately 3,000 merger cases decided during the first fifteen years of the Merger Regulation's regime, only fifteen have been blocked.

More frequently, the Commission imposes **conditions** on the **structuring** of a proposed deal in order to give its clearance. In a 2001 Notice on Remedies Acceptable under Regulation 4064/89, the Commission provided some guidance on what it would consider appropriate, such as partial divestiture in order to create or strengthen competition.

The formal criteria of the Merger Regulation may in practice be supplemented by other considerations, such as industrial policy concerns or the like.

9.31 Is EC competition law also binding for state-owned or specially privileged enterprises?

Although competition law is not applicable to activities connected with the exercise of official powers, as the ECJ held in the

Eurocontrol Case (→9.6), Article 86(1) TEC clearly provides that with regard to 'public undertakings and undertakings to which Member States grant special or exclusive rights', Member States shall not enact any measures contrary to the Treaty's competition law rules. In Cases 188–190/80 *France, Italy and the United Kingdom* v. *Commission* [1982] ECR 2545, the ECJ accepted the Community legislator's definition of 'public undertaking' as 'any undertaking over which the public authorities may exercise directly or indirectly a dominant influence', for instance, if they 'hold the major part of the undertaking's subscribed capital, control the majority of the votes, or can appoint more than half of the members of its administrative, managerial or supervisory body'.

An illustration of the ECJ's approach to Article 86(1) TEC can be found in Case 18/88 *RTT* v. *GB-Inno-BM SA* [1991] ECR 5941. In that case, the Court found that Article 86(1) TEC, in conjunction with Article 82 TEC, 'preclude[s] a Member State from granting to the undertaking which operates the public telecommunications network the power to lay down standards for telephone equipment and to check that economic operators meet those standards when it is itself competing with those operators on the market of that equipment'.

? 9.32 Are there special competition law rules for utilities or other services in the general interest?

In most Member States, certain businesses of general economic interest, such as postal, electricity, information and other services, are granted exclusive rights in order to compensate for their service obligations in non-profitable areas. The EC Treaty accepts this practice in the rather ambiguous Article 86(2) TEC which provides:

> Undertakings entrusted with the operation of services of general economic interest or having the character of a revenue-producing monopoly shall be subject to the rules contained in this Treaty, in particular to the rules on competition, insofar as the application of such rules does not obstruct the performance, in law or in fact, of the particular tasks assigned to them. The development of trade must not be affected to such an extent as would be contrary to the interests of the Community.

Although the ECJ has interpreted this exception restrictively, it upheld it in case of firms with universal or quasi-universal service obligations. It thereby prevented private sector competitors from exploiting the profitable parts of an activity since this would make it financially impossible for the public service provider to fulfil its tasks. This was the main reasoning for the ECJ in the *Corbeau* Case, Case C-320/91 *Criminal proceedings against Paul Corbeau* [1993] ECR I-2533, where the Court upheld the Belgian postal monopoly which prevented a competitor operating a fast delivery service.

The Article 86(2) TEC defence was also successfully invoked in Case C-475/99 *Ambulanz Glöckner* v. *Landkreis Südwestpfalz* [2001] ECR I-8089, where the court held that this provision 'allows Member States to confer, on undertakings to which they entrust the operation of services of general economic interest, exclusive rights which may hinder the application of the rules of the Treaty on competition insofar as restrictions on competition, or even the exclusion of all competition, by other economic operators are necessary to ensure the performance of the particular tasks assigned to the undertakings holding the exclusive rights'. In the particular case, the exclusive right to provide a profitable service in the field of non-emergency ambulance transports was given to a firm which also provided emergency transports that were not profitable.

9.33 Does the Treaty prohibit Member States granting subsidies to private companies?

Article 87(1) TEC provides that:

> any aid granted by a Member State or through State resources in any form whatsoever which distorts or threatens to distort competition by favouring certain undertakings or the production of certain goods shall, insofar as it affects trade between Member States, be incompatible with the common market.

Article 87(2) TEC, however, does exempt the following types of subsidies:

(a) aid having a social character, granted to individual consumers, provided that such aid is granted without discrimination related to the origin of the products concerned;

(b) aid to make good the damage caused by natural disasters or exceptional occurrences; and

(c) aid granted to the economy of certain areas of the Federal Republic of Germany affected by the division of Germany, insofar as such aid is required in order to compensate for the economic disadvantages caused by that division.

While the Treaty does not define what constitutes 'state aid', the notion of aid used by the Commission and the European courts closely follows the GATT/WTO concept of a subsidy (→ *11.2*). Thus, in order to qualify as 'aid' a measure must confer an economic or financial advantage upon an undertaking. A benefit may also consist in tax holidays or reduced public charges, preferential interest rates or other advantageous loan conditions. There will be no 'financial advantage' where payments are received to offset public service obligations. Thus,

in Case C-280/00 *Altmark Trans GmbH* [2003] ECR I-7747, the
ECJ held that:

> where a State measure must be regarded as compensation
> for the services provided by the recipient undertakings
> in order to discharge public service obligations, so
> that those undertakings do not enjoy a real financial
> advantage and the measure does not have the effect of
> putting them in a more favourable competitive position
> than the undertakings competing with them, such a
> measure is not caught by [Article 87(1)] of the Treaty.

The advantage must be granted by a Member State or
'through State resources' which is broadly interpreted. In order
to assess state participation in undertakings a market investor
test is applied. According to the *Tubemeuse* Case, Case C-142/87
Belgium v. *Commission* [1990] ECR I-959, 'to determine whether
such measures are in the nature of State aid, the relevant cri-
terion is . . . whether the undertaking could have obtained the
amounts in question on the capital market'. Prohibited aid must
be 'specific' (Article 87 TEC speaks of 'favouring certain undertakings or the production of certain goods'), which implies that
measures broadly benefiting all market operators are usually
not aid.

Article 87(3) TEC further provides that the following types
of subsidies may be declared compatible with the Common
Market by the Commission:

> (a) aid to promote the economic development of areas
>   where the standard of living is abnormally low or
>   where there is serious underemployment;
> (b) aid to promote the execution of an important project
>   of common European interest or to remedy a serious
>   disturbance in the economy of a Member State;
> (c) aid to facilitate the development of certain economic
>   activities or of certain economic areas, where such

aid does not adversely affect trading conditions to an extent contrary to the common interest;

(d) aid to promote culture and heritage conservation where such aid does not affect trading conditions and competition in the Community to an extent that is contrary to the common interest; and

(e) such other categories of aid as may be specified by decision of the Council acting by a qualified majority on a proposal from the Commission.

In this way, Article 87 TEC clearly attempts to complement the competition law rules addressed to private undertakings by proscribing state measures which would equally distort competition on the Common Market.

10 Selected Community policies

The initial **European Economic Community** was largely about the creation of a **Common Market**, comprising a customs union and providing for the unhampered free movement of goods, persons, services and capital. Over the years, Community competences have been considerably **extended** into other fields, called **policies** in EC jargon. This chapter will briefly address those Community policies which have gained significantly in importance, such as the **Common Agricultural Policy (CAP)**, **environmental** and **social policy**, with particular regard to **non-discrimination** issues. All were hardly visible in the original TEC and grew only as a consequence of **judge-made** law, Community **legislation** and **Treaty amendments**.

10.1 What are the objectives of the CAP?

According to Article 33(1) TEC the aims of CAP are:

 (a) to increase productivity;
 (b) to ensure a fair standard of living for the agricultural community;
 (c) to stabilise markets;
 (d) to ensure the availability of supplies; and
 (e) to ensure reasonable prices for consumers.

Under the so-called *lex specialis* principle, which provides that specialised rules prevail over more general ones, CAP rules take precedence over other Treaty rules, such as those on the free movement of goods. According to Article 32(1) TEC, the CAP applies to agricultural products defined as 'products of the soil, of stockfarming and of fisheries and products of first-stage processing directly related to these products'.

10.2 What principles is the CAP based on?

By the time of the Stresa Conference in 1958 the following principles of the CAP were laid down:

- single market/market unity (replacing national markets via free movement);
- Community preference (through import regulating instruments, subsidies and other measures); and
- financial solidarity (transfer payments between states involving net-payers vs. net receivers, the creation of the European Agricultural Guidance and Guarantee Fund, within which the Guidance Section finances structural measures and the Guarantee Section finances common market organisations).

10.3 How is the CAP put into operation?

Article 34 TEC provides for the creation of 'a common organisation of agricultural markets', which may include the 'regulation of prices, aids for the production and marketing of the various products, storage and carryover arrangements and common machinery for stabilizing imports or exports'.

Such **Common Market Organisations** were created for **different products** (for example, cereals, oil seeds and protein crops, beef and veal, dairy products and others), which typically provided for both **external protection** in the form of levies, increasing the cheaper import price to the threshold price set by the Community, as well as for **internal intervention** arrangements according to which agencies had to buy if the market price fell under a pre-set intervention price. This costly system clearly guaranteed a minimum income to producers. In practice, most of the enormous CAP spending, which in 2000 accounted for almost half of the entire Community expenses, supports the income of European farmers.

 ## 10.4 Is there an end in sight for CAP reform?

A major **CAP reform** was initiated in 1992, which, among other things, **reduced guaranteed prices**, provided for compensatory payments on the basis of factors of production, not of production, foresaw early retirement schemes for farmers, offered set-aside premiums for taking agricultural land out of production and encouraged the restructuring of farms and ecological concerns. In 1997, CAP reform plans were re-emphasised in the **AGENDA 2000**, which proposed further price support cuts and a shift to direct aid for farmers.

A number of these plans were adopted in the 2003 reform which provided for the payment of subsidies independently of the volume of production. So-called 'single farm payments' were linked to respecting environmental, food safety and animal welfare standards. In 2008, this CAP reform was subjected to a 'health check' assessing its effect and trying to reinforce the plan to reduce market intervention by the EC.

10.5 What does the Mulder case stand for?

The *Mulder* Case illustrates the difficulties of implementing CAP principles when they collide with general principles of EC law (→ *ch. 6*) and may trigger the Community's non-contractual liability (→ *4.9*).

The case arose from an attempt to reduce the excess production of milk in the Community. In the first *Mulder* Case, Case 120/86 *Mulder* v. *Minister van Landbouw en Visserij* [1988] ECR 2321, a Dutch farmer, who had agreed not to market milk for a five-year period, applied for a production quota after that period. The Dutch authorities rejected his request because under Dutch implementing legislation, based on a 1984 Council Regulation, quotas were issued on the basis of the production levels of the previous year. In a preliminary reference from an action against the Dutch authorities, the ECJ held this to be a violation of the producer's legitimate expectations and annulled the Council Regulation (→ *6.5*). In the second *Mulder* Case, Joined Cases C-104/89 and 37/90 *Mulder* v. *Council and Commission* [1992] ECR I-3061, the ECJ found an entitlement to lost profits on the basis of Article 288(2) TEC which provides that:

> in the case of non-contractual liability, the Community shall, in accordance with the general principles common to the laws of the Member States, make good any damage caused by its institutions or by its servants in the performance of their duties.

10.6 Does the EC have its own fisheries policy?

The Common Fisheries Policy is part of CAP. The first Common Market Organisation for Fish was established in 1970. It provides for marketing standards (quality controls), a producer organisation and the setting of guide prices by the Community (if the market price falls below withdrawal prices production is withdrawn from sale).

The Common Fisheries Policy is based on the principle of non-discrimination between Community nationals with regard to access to fishing grounds, except for a 12-mile coastal band reserved for local fishers. It further provides for conservation measures, expressed in annually fixed 'total allowable catches', which are in turn divided among the Member States in the form of quotas for specific fish species.

10.7 How did environmental protection in the Community start?

Since the 1972 EC Paris summit, which coincided with the UN Stockholm Conference on the Environment, five-year non-binding 'Environmental Action Programmes' have been adopted by the Parliament and the Council. What was initially a mere 'service' in the Commission for environmental and consumer issues subsequently became a Directorate-General for the Environment, Nuclear Safety and Civil Protection and is now the Environment Directorate-General supporting the Commissioner for Environment.

10.8 What is the legal basis for Community legislation on the environment?

The legal basis for the Community's environmental legislation is complex and has been subject to numerous amendments. Before the inclusion of express environmental powers by the SEA 1986, the harmonisation of the laws of Member States provided for in Article 100 (now Article 94) TEC and the Community's

implied powers clause of Article 235 (now Article 308) TEC
($\rightarrow 3.1$) served as legal basis for the EC's early environmental
legislation. The practical drawback of both provisions was that
they required unanimity ($\rightarrow 2.5$), which involved the danger of
simply reaching the lowest common denominator. The SEA
introduced a title on environment that included Article 130s
(now Article 175) TEC, which required unanimity but authorised the Council to define (unanimously) those matters on which
decisions were to be taken by a qualified majority. Article 130t
(now Article 176) TEC contained a safeguard clause according
to which Community measures 'shall not prevent any Member
State from maintaining or introducing more stringent protective measures' compatible with the Treaty.

Under the Maastricht Treaty, environmental legislation
became subject to the Article 252 TEC procedure, which requires
a qualified majority and co-operation with the European
Parliament ($\rightarrow 3.6$). Today, environmental legislation is subject
to the co-decision procedure of Article 251 TEC ($\rightarrow 3.7$).

10.9 Give examples of Community legislation in the environmental field

Since the 1970s, the EC has adopted an impressively wide range
of environmental legislation, mostly in the form of directives,
aiming at harmonisation instead of unification brought about
by regulations.

The main focus of Community legislation has been on com-
bating pollution and environmental damage, through clean
water objectives (by limiting discharge of dangerous substances),
clean air legislation (through limiting sulphur dioxide, lead and
other pollutants), noise reduction (for example, lawnmowers),
risk control for chemicals and biotechnology, as well as on
nature and resources conservation, through banning pesticides,

adopting the wild birds directive and various waste management directives since 1975, and by becoming signatory to international environmental agreements such as the 1989 Basle Convention concerning cross-border movements of dangerous waste.

In 1985, Directive 85/337 introduced an 'environmental impact assessment' procedure requiring a preventive policy approach for public and private projects.

? 10.10 What are the principles of EC environmental action?

According to Article 174(1) TEC, the Community's environmental policy pursues the objectives of 'preserving, protecting and improving the quality of the environment; protecting human health; prudent and rational utilization of natural resources; promoting measures at international level to deal with regional or worldwide environmental problems'.

Article 174(2) TEC further ensures that:

> Community policy on the environment shall aim at a high level of protection taking into account the diversity of situations in the various regions of the Community. It shall be based on the precautionary principle and on the principles that preventive action should be taken, that environmental damage should as a priority be rectified at source and that the polluter should pay.

? 10.11 Under what conditions are Member States permitted to adopt environmental rules that might restrict the free movement of goods?

In the so-called *Danish Beverage Container* Case, Case 302/86 *Commission* v. *Denmark* [1988] ECR 4607, the Commission instituted an infringement action against Denmark because it considered the Danish deposit and return system for drink containers to be contrary to the free movement of goods ($\rightarrow$ *ch. 7*). The Danish return system for beer and soft drink containers had two distinctive features: first, marketing was permitted only in re-usable containers that had to be approved by a national agency; and second, non-approved containers could be used by foreign producers for up to 3,000 hectolitres with a deposit-and-return system. Building on its judgment in the *Cassis* Case ($\rightarrow$ *7.5*), the ECJ held that:

> in the absence of common rules relating to the marketing of the products in question, obstacles to free movement within the Community resulting from disparities between the national laws must be accepted insofar as such rules are, applicable to domestic and imported products without distinction, may be recognized as being necessary in order to satisfy mandatory requirements recognized by Community law. Such rules must be proportionate to the aim in view.

On that basis, the Court concluded that environmental protection was a mandatory requirement and that the deposit-and-return system was proportionate. The restriction of the quantity of imported products inherent in the system for non-approved containers, however, was disproportionate.

? 10.12 What was the so-called Walloon Waste Case?

In Case C-2/90 *Commission* v. *Belgium* [1992] ECR I-4431, the Belgian region of Wallonia restricted the import of foreign non-toxic waste and prohibited its deposit there. These rules violated a directive as far as hazardous waste was concerned. With regard to non-hazardous waste, which was not covered by common Community rules, the Court found that they

contravened Article 28 TEC (→ *7.3*), but that they were justified as 'mandatory requirements' (→ *7.5*) even if discriminatory. In fact, the ECJ apparently dispensed with the element of
discrimination inherent in an import ban by asserting rather
cryptically that:

> taking into account differences between waste produced
> in one place and that produced in another and of the
> link between waste and the place of its production,
> the challenged measures cannot be considered
> discriminatory.

10.13 What kind of activities has the Community undertaken in the field of consumer protection?

Consumer protection was introduced into the TEC by the 1992
Maastricht Treaty which in Article 129a(2) TEC authorised specific action under the co-decision procedure (→*3.7*). Previously,
consumer protection legislation consisted mainly of harmonisation measures, although the First Consumer Protection
Action Programme had been adopted in 1975. It provided for
basic consumer rights, covering, for example, health and safety
protection, the protection of economic and legal interests,
the right of redress, the right to information and the right of
representation.

The 1986 SEA introduced the notion of the consumer into the
Treaty. Article 100a TEC entitled the Commission to propose
measures designed to protect consumers, taking as a base a
'high level of protection'. Today, Article 153(1) TEC mandates
the Community to:

> contribute to protecting the health, safety and economic
> interests of consumers, as well as to promoting their right

to information, education and to organise themselves in order to safeguard their interests.

In particular in the health and safety area, important standards for consumer products were laid down in numerous directives, such as Directive 85/734 on Defective Products or Directive 92/59 on General Product Safety. With regard to the economic and legal interests of consumers, directives on misleading advertising, door-step sales, product liability, consumer credit, package holidays, unfair terms in consumer contracts and other issues have been adopted.

10.14 What is the legal basis for the Community's social policy legislation?

The Social Policy Chapter of the Treaty, starting with Article 136 TEC, does not contain general legislative powers for the Community. Rather, according to Article 137(1) TEC it is mostly intended to 'support and complement the activities of the Member States in [various] fields'.

For a long time, Community action in the field of social policy was thus based on general harmonisation legislation, such as a number of directives adopted under (old) Article 100 TEC which required unanimity in the Council and consultation of the Parliament ($\rightarrow$ 3.5). The 1986 SEA introduced (old) Article 118a TEC, which expressly mentioned a legislative competence in the field of 'health and safety of workers'. This is the core of the current Article 137 TEC power of the Community to adopt minimum requirements by way of directives, some of which are adopted according to the co-decision procedure ($\rightarrow$ 3.7), while others are adopted pursuant to the consultation procedure ($\rightarrow$ 3.5).

With regard to workers' health and safety, working conditions, the integration of persons excluded from the labour market, the information and consultation of workers, equality between men and women with regard to labour market opportunities and treatment at work, the Council may adopt directives by qualified majority in co-decision with the Parliament and after consulting the Economic and Social Committee and the Committee of the Regions. Measures in the areas of social security and social protection of workers, protection of workers where their employment contract is terminated, representation and collective defence of the interests of workers and employers, conditions of employment for third country nationals legally residing in Community territory, financial contributions for promotion of employment and job creation may be adopted unanimously after consulting the Parliament and the Committees.

The 1997 Amsterdam Treaty also added specific legislative powers in the field of **anti-discrimination law**. The new Article 141(3) TEC gives the Council the power to adopt measures in the field of 'equal opportunities and equal treatment of men and women in matters of employment and occupation' beyond the strict 'equal pay' principle laid down in Article 141(1) TEC (→ *10.17*).

In addition, a new Article 13 TEC permits the adoption of provisions on **non-discrimination**, and authorises the Council, acting unanimously, to 'take appropriate action to combat any discrimination based on sex, race, ethnic origin, religion or belief, disability, age or sexual orientation'.

? 10.15 Describe the major results of the Social Action Programme 1974

In common with other policy areas, the Community used its harmonisation competence in order to adopt various social policy goals. The measures taken pursuant to the 1974 Social

Policy Programme are a good example of such Community legislation aimed at fighting unemployment. The programme led to three particularly important directives:

* Directive 75/129 on **collective redundancies** which requires advance (thirty days) notice for mass lay-offs (10% of the workforce), as well as for 'consultations' with workers' representatives leading to possible government-proposed 'solutions';
* Directive 77/187 on the **safeguarding of employees' rights** in the event of **transfer of undertakings**, businesses, or parts of businesses, now codified in Directive 2001/23, which entitles employees to keep their employment relationship when all or part of the entity by which they were employed is transferred; and
* Directive 80/987 on the **protection of employees** in the event of **insolvency** of their employer, the famous '*Francovich* directive' ($\rightarrow 4.9$), which requires the setting up of 'guarantee institutions' with assets independent of the employers' capital to provide for payment of wages and benefits for a certain period after insolvency.

10.16 What is the Community's Social Charter?

This **non-binding instrument** was adopted at the Strasbourg European Council in 1989 as the '**Community Charter of the Fundamental Social Rights of Workers**'. Its objectives were to be translated into proposals in a Commission Action Plan, which led to a number of Council **directives** on health and safety standards, mutual recognition and other issues. The Community's Social Charter should not be confused with the 1961 European Social Charter of the Council of Europe, which is equally referred to in Article 136 TEC as a source of inspiration for EU social policy measures.

The Community's Social Charter was transformed into a binding Protocol on Social Policy added to the Maastricht Treaty to promote employment, improve working conditions and foster dialogue between management and labour, etc. The Social Policy Protocol contained complicated decision-making provisions with special qualified majority quorums because, initially, the UK abstained from it ($\rightarrow$ *1.6*). With the Treaty of Amsterdam the Protocol was incorporated into the TEC and now forms the new Title XI, Articles 136–145 TEC.

10.17 May an individual rely directly upon the 'equal pay' principle contained in Article 141 TEC?

Article 141(1) TEC provides that 'each Member State shall ensure that the principle of equal pay for male and female workers for equal work or work of equal value is applied'. However, the wording of this Treaty provision was not always that clear and precise and, thus, gave rise to questions as to its direct effect. The old Article 119(1) TEC was formulated as follows: 'Each Member State shall during the first stage ensure and subsequently maintain the application of the principle that men and women should receive equal pay for equal work.'

In a landmark decision in 1976, Case 43/75 *Defrenne* v. *Sabena* [1976] ECR 455 ($\rightarrow$ *4.5, 5.10*), the ECJ held that – after the first stage which had expired in December 1961 and despite its language – this provision had 'horizontal direct effect' in cases of 'direct and overt discrimination'. According to the ECJ:

> the principle that men and women should receive equal
> pay, which is laid down in Article 119, may be relied
> on before national courts. These courts have a duty to
> ensure the protection of the rights which that provision

vests in individuals, in particular in the case of those forms of discrimination which have their origin in legislative provisions or collective labour agreements, as well as where men and women receive unequal pay for equal work which is carried out in the same establishment or service, whether private or public.

10.18 What exactly is covered by the concept of 'equal pay' in Article 141 TEC?

Since 'pay' is not defined in the Treaty it was left to the ECJ to determine the scope of the equal pay principle. The Court, not surprisingly, has arrived at a rather broad definition regarding any consideration that a worker receives directly or indirectly in respect of employment from his or her employer as 'pay'. In its case law, the ECJ has qualified as 'pay', among other things, travel concessions (Case 12/81 *Garland* v. *British Rail Engineering* [1982] ECR 359), pension schemes (Case 170/84 *Bilka-Kaufhaus GmbH* v. *Karin Weber von Hartz* [1986] ECR 1607), redundancy payments (Case C-262/88 *Barber* v. *Guardian Royal Exchange Assurance Group* [1990] ECR I-1889), maternity pay (Case C-342 *Gillespie* v. *Northern Health and Social Services Board* [1996] ECR I-457), and compensation for unfair dismissal (Case C-167/97 *R.* v. *Secretary of State for Employment, ex parte Seymour-Smith and Perez* [1999] ECR I-623).

10.19 Outline the major Community acts of the EC's non-discrimination legislation

Initially, most Community legislation in the field of non-discrimination related to gender discrimination, such as the Equal Pay, the Equal Treatment, and the Social Security Directive.

The so-called **Equal Pay Directive** 75/117 basically implemented Article 119 (now 141) TEC. It specified the concept of 'equal work' including 'work of equal value' which was not covered by the old Article 119 TEC, but is now covered by Article 141 TEC. Article 1(1) of the Directive provides:

> The principle of equal pay for men and women outlined in Article 119 of the Treaty, hereinafter called 'principle of equal pay', means, for the same work or for work to which equal value is attributed, the elimination of all discrimination on grounds of sex with regard to all aspects and conditions of remuneration.

The **Equal Treatment Directive**, Directive 76/207, amended by Directive 2002/73, covers 'hiring, promotion, all working conditions, and vocational training'. Its Article 2(1) provided that:

> For the purposes of the following provisions, the principle of equal treatment shall mean that there shall be no discrimination whatsoever on grounds of sex either directly or indirectly by reference in particular to marital or family status.

Similar equal treatment provisions can be found in Directive 86/613 regarding those who are self-employed.

In 2006, these separate directives were replaced by a single **gender discrimination directive**, Directive 2006/54 on the implementation of the principle of equal opportunities and equal treatment of men and women in matters of employment and occupation, which left the substance largely unchanged.

The **Social Security Directive**, Directive 79/7, extends non-discrimination to the fields of social security and social protection to workers and in Directive 86/378 to the self-employed.

In addition, the Community has legislated against race and ethnic discrimination in the so-called **Race Directive**, Directive 2000/43, and against various other forms of discrimination on the basis of religion, belief, disability, age and sexual orientation in the so-called **Framework Directive**, Directive 2000/78 establishing a general framework for equal treatment in employment and occupation.

> **10.20 Does the general exclusion of part-time employees from an employer's private pension plan constitute indirect discrimination if most part-time employees are women?**

Sometimes, rules and regulations which appear neutral on their face may constitute indirect discrimination, if, *de facto*, they primarily affect members of a particular group. According to Article 2(2) of the **Equal Treatment Directive**, Directive 76/207 amended by Directive 2002/73:

> indirect discrimination shall be taken to occur where an apparently neutral provision, criterion or practice would put persons of [a protected group] at a particular disadvantage compared with other persons, unless that provision, criterion or practice is objectively justified by a legitimate aim and the means of achieving that aim are appropriate and necessary.

As this legislative definition demonstrates, there is a specific justification for some forms of indirect discrimination, that is, if they serve legitimate aims and fulfil a proportionality test.

Since women are more likely to be part-time employees than men, any provisions favouring full-time over part-time employees regularly result in forms of indirect discrimination. This conclusion was drawn by the Court on the basis of Article 141 TEC (the old 119 TEC) and not the Directive in Case 170/84 *Bilka-Kaufhaus GmbH* v. *Karin Weber von Hartz* [1986] ECR 1607. There, the ECJ held that a private pension plan constituted 'pay' in the sense of Article 141 and that the exclusion of part-time workers from it might infringe Article 141 'where that exclusion affects a far greater number of women than men, unless the undertaking shows that the exclusion is based on objectively justified factors unrelated to any discrimination on grounds of sex'. (This shift of the burden of proof has been codified in Directive 97/80/EC on the burden of proof in cases of discrimination based on sex.) However, the Court acknowledged that the measure might pursue a legitimate aim if it was intended to have staff working at all times including weekends and evenings. Similarly, in Case 96/80 *Jenkins* v. *Kingsgate* [1981] ECR 911, the ECJ found that a lower wage for part-time than for full-time workers was not an illicit discrimination *per se*. Rather, where more women were affected than men, it might be lawful through an 'objective justification' which could lie in an incentive to take up full-time employment.

? 10.21 Are discriminatory employment practices always contrary to Community law?

EU non-discrimination legislation aims at eliminating discrimination. Nevertheless, it recognises that in certain circumstances, discriminatory practices may be justified. For instance, the 1976 Equal Treatment Directive – like the Race Directive and the Framework Directive (→ *10.19*) – provides that differences in treatment may be justified 'where, by reason of the nature of the particular occupational activities concerned or of the context in which they are carried out, such a characteristic constitutes a genuine and determining occupational requirement'. This provision permits a theatre to hire exclusively females for the role of a tragic heroine or the Catholic Church to employ only Catholics as priests.

The boundaries of the 'genuine occupational requirement' have been tested in a number of cases concerning access to the armed forces by women. In Case C-273/97 *Sirdar* v. *Army Board and Secretary of State for Defence* [1999] ECR I-7403, the ECJ upheld the exclusion of women from a segment of the UK armed forces, the Royal Marines, because this army group had a policy that every member had to have the ability to fight at any time. In a very controversial judgment, in Case C-285/98 *Kreil* v. *Germany* [2000] ECR I-69, however, the Court held that German constitutional law barring women outright from army jobs involving the use of arms was contrary to the Community principle of equal treatment for men and women. While the Court found that derogations remained possible where sex constituted a determining factor for access to certain special combat units, it held that a general exclusion of women was a disproportionate discrimination.

10.22 Does Community law permit positive discrimination in the sense of affirmative action programmes?

One of the most difficult and controversial issues of non-discrimination law is the question of whether and to what extent the law should permit temporary discrimination in favour of historically disadvantaged groups in order to achieve an equality of results. Particularly, as regards hiring practices systems favouring the under-represented sex or race which have been used in many states in various affirmative action programmes.

Their legitimacy was recognised in Article 2(4) of the 1976 Equal Treatment Directive (→ *10.19*), which provided an exception to the general equal treatment principle in respect of measures intended 'to promote equal opportunity for men and women, in particular by removing existing inequalities which affect women's opportunities'. The 1997 Amsterdam Treaty inserted a new paragraph 4 to Article 141 TEC which clarifies that Member States may maintain or adopt:

measures providing for specific advantages in order to make it easier for the under-represented sex to pursue a vocational activity or to prevent or compensate for disadvantages in professional careers.

In Case C- 450/93 *Kalanke* v. *Freie Hansestadt Bremen* [1995] ECR I-3051, the ECJ held, however, that such affirmative action measures may not take the form of strict quotas or include a system whereby a job would automatically go to a woman in cases of equal qualification. In Case C-409/95 *Hellmut Marschall* v. *Land Nordrhein-Westfalen* [1997] ECR I-6363, the ECJ stated that a qualification introduced by a saving clause which enabled male candidates to be made the subject of an objective assessment excluded absolute and unconditional priority for women. The Court concluded that priority given to equally qualified women – which was designed to restore the balance – was not contrary to Community law provided that an objective assessment of each individual candidate, irrespective of the sex of the candidate in question, was assured and that the promotion of a male candidate was not excluded from the outset.

This case law was confirmed in Case C-407/98 *Abrahamsson and Anderson* v. *Fogelqvist* [2000] ECR I-5539. In that case the Court held that Swedish legislation which automatically favoured access for women to public posts, even where their qualifications were not equal to those of their male candidates, was contrary to Community law. The Court pointed out that priority for women where their qualifications were equal – as a way of restoring balance – was not contrary to Community law provided that an objective assessment of each candidature was guaranteed.

10.23 Is an earlier retirement age for women than for men contrary to Community law?

Social security questions, and in particular pension schemes, are frequently the result of very controversial public policy choices of the various Member States. Thus, such issues were initially considered to be outside the reach of EC law. Article 119 (now Article 141) TEC originally covered only 'pay', and even secondary EC law such as the Social Security Directive 79/7 (→ *10.19*) expressly provided in its Article 7 that states might 'exclude from its scope the determination of pensionable age'.

Nevertheless, different **retirement ages** soon became the subject of litigation before the ECJ and the Court gradually acted more assertively in its scrutiny. In Case 19/81 *Burton* v. *British Railways Board* [1982] ECR 555, a case concerning a man who alleged discrimination on receiving lower redundancy dismissal benefits than women at the same age, the ECJ held that a private plan, paralleling the state social security system as far as different pensionable age was concerned, did not violate equal treatment.

In 1986, however, the ECJ held that different retirement ages were unlawful in Case 152/84 *Marshall* v. *Southampton and SW Hampshire Area Health Authority* [1986] ECR 723, a leading case denying horizontal direct effect and limiting it to the vertical relationship between individuals and Member States (→ *4.8*). Marshall complained that she had been discriminatorily dismissed at age 62, while men were retired at 65. According to the ECJ, Article 5(1) of the Equal Treatment Directive 76/207, regulating 'working conditions, including the conditions governing dismissal', 'must be interpreted as meaning that a general policy concerning dismissal involving the dismissal of a woman solely because she has attained the qualifying age for a state pension, which age is different under national legislation for men and women, constitutes discrimination on grounds of sex, contrary to that directive'. The Court had first found that the case did not concern access to a retirement scheme, which would probably have been covered by the Social Security Directive 79/7, but rather the fixing of an age limit pursuant to a general policy concerning dismissal, which was covered by the Equal Treatment Directive.

Finally, in Case C-262/88 *Barber* v. *Guardian Royal Exchange Assurance Group* [1990] I-1889, the Court found 'an age condition which differs according to sex in respect of pensions paid under a contracted-out scheme [early retirement pension for men at age 55, women at age 50], even if the difference between the pensionable age for men and that for women is based on the one provided for by the national statutory scheme' contrary to Article 141 requiring 'equal pay'. The case concerned a man who was dismissed at age 52 and who did not receive an early retirement pension because it was generally offered to men at the age of 55. Because such an early retirement pension was generally offered to women at the age of 50 he successfully sued for discrimination.

It should be noted that **age discrimination** is now included in the abovementioned Framework Directive, Directive 2000/78 (→ *10.19*).

11   The EC and the EU as international actors

One of the main achievements of the 2004 **Draft Constitution Treaty** in its endeavour to simplify European law and, thus, to make it more accessible to EU citizens, would have been the **abolition** of the **three pillars** under the common EU roof. Instead, **one single EU** would have replaced the existing supranational EC. The Union would have pursued both the supranational Community policies as well as the inter-governmental areas of cooperation, such as the CFSP. Also on the international plane, it would have simplified matters because one EU, endowed with **international legal personality** in Article I-7 CT, would have been able to enter into **international agreements** with third countries and international organisations. Alas, as things stand now, the adoption of both the Constitution Treaty and the Lisbon Reform Treaty remains unlikely and we have to live with the current complicated structures of an **EC**, acting on the international level mainly in the field of **external trade** and concluding various treaties touching upon Community powers, as well as an **EU**, trying to keep the Member States within the framework of the commonly agreed upon **CFSP** and within very limited powers of its own.

This final chapter tries to provide a brief overview of the different aspects of the activities of the EC/EU on the international plane.

11.1 What is the legal basis of the Community's external relations?

The **external relations** of the EC were traditionally limited to **trade relations** with third countries, conducted either on the basis of unilateral measures, such as anti-dumping or countervailing duties, or through trade agreements. For both types of 'external' activities, the **Common Commercial Policy (CCP)** powers expressly mentioned in Article 133 TEC provided a solid legal basis (→ *11.2*). The other traditional Community competence concerning external relations is the power found in Article 310 TEC to enter into **association agreements,** which are frequently pre-accession relations going beyond mere trade relations (→ *11.11–13*). These agreements should not be confused with the association with overseas countries and territories of Member States, such as Greenland, French Polynesia or the British Virgin Islands, provided for in Article 182 TEC. Parallel to the extension of the Community's internal competences, its **treaty-making power** was gradually extended to include research and technology, environment and development policy (since the 1986 SEA), monetary and foreign exchange matters, education, culture, health and trans-European networks (since the 1992 Maastricht Treaty). Also the Amsterdam and the Nice Treaty amendments further extended these express powers. Moreover, Article 302 TEC states that the Commission maintains appropriate relations with the UN and other **international organisations** (→ *2.14*).

   In addition to these express powers, the ECJ developed a rather complex case law of so-called **implied external powers,** outlined below (→ *11.5–10*).

? 11.2 How does the EC pursue its CCP?

The Community's activities under Article 133 TEC are not limited to treaty-making powers with regard to trade matters. Rather, they also cover **unilateral external trade measures**, such as the imposition of a **common customs tariff**, Community rules on **anti-dumping** and **countervailing duties** against **subsidies**, as well as other **trade measures**. The establishment of a **common external tariff** is one of the essential features of the European customs union, and it involves applying uniform customs duties to products imported from third countries ($\rightarrow$ 7.1). The customs union envisaged in the original 1957 EEC Treaty and completed in 1968 requires the elimination of all customs duties and restrictions among the Member States of the Community and the introduction of a common customs tariff (an external tariff which applies to third-country goods).

Since 1988 the imposition of a Community-wide common customs tariff has been based on the so-called 'combined nomenclature', originally laid down in Council Regulation (EEC) 2658/87 of 23 July 1987 on the tariff and statistical nomenclature and on the common customs tariff. This combined nomenclature classifies goods for customs and statistical purposes. Every year the Commission adopts a Regulation reproducing a complete version of the combined nomenclature and common customs tariff duty rates.

In addition, the EC's external trade is regulated by a number of **unilateral** measures **restricting** the import (such as safeguard measures) or **export** of goods (such as restrictions covering radioactive waste or culturally, artistically or historically important products). Unilateral export restrictions are also laid down in Regulation 1334/2000 for so-called dual use goods, that is, products that may serve military purposes in addition to their primary civilian use.

According to the **Anti-dumping Regulation** 384/96, which implements the relevant 1994 GATT code, anti-dumping duties may be imposed on imported products if they are dumped, that is, **sold below** their **normal value**, and such dumping causes **injury** to a Community **industry**.

Pursuant to **Regulation 2026/97** on common rules for **protection** against **subsidised imports** from countries which are not members of the European Community, the Community may also take trade measures against subsidies granted by foreign states to their exporters which cause harm to European producers. A **subsidy**, or 'state aid' in Community terminology (→ *9.33*), is defined as a **financial contribution** by a government or any other **public body** which **confers a benefit**. Examples of less obvious subsidies are, for instance, tax holidays, export credits, or transport benefits. The Community's CCP power to adopt measures against subsidised imports from third countries, usually in the form of so-called countervailing duties, should not be confused with the rules on state aid in Articles 87–89 TEC, which prohibit Member States from subsidising firms and thereby distort competition within the Common Market (→ *9.33*).

Finally, the EC may also counteract other 'obstacles to trade' on the basis of the so-called **Trade Barriers Regulation** 3286/94, which provides for the initiation of dispute settlement under the WTO rules, the imposition of duties or quotas and the like.

? 11.3 How does the Community enter into international agreements?

According to the standard treaty-making procedure laid down in Article 300 TEC, the **Commission**, upon authorisation from the Council, conducts treaty **negotiations** with third states or organisations, while the Council – after having consulted the European Parliament – concludes international agreements acting on the basis of qualified majority (→ *3.5*).

Special rules apply for certain types of agreements. In the case of free trade agreements on the basis of Article 133 TEC, the Commission negotiates in consultation with a special Council Committee (comitology), the so-called Article 133 Committee (→ *3.8*, *4.12*, *7.1*). In the case of association agreements (→ *11.11–13*) and agreements covering fields for which unanimity is required for the adoption of internal rules, the Council has to act unanimously. Further, association agreements and other important treaties, such as those setting up a specific institutional framework or having important budgetary implications, require the assent of the European Parliament (→ *3.8*).

11.4 Was the Commission competent to conclude an international agreement involving competition law?

In the division of powers system of the EC, it is the task of the Commission to negotiate and of the Council to conclude international agreements. The Commission's own 'treaty-making power' is strictly limited to privileges and immunities according to the Privileges and Immunities Protocol and 'administrative agreements' with the UN and other international organisations according to Article 302 TEC.

Thus, as a consequence, in Case 327/91 *France* v. *Commission* [1994] ECR I-3641, the ECJ struck down a 1991 EC–US agreement for mutual cooperation and assistance in matters of antitrust enforcement concluded by the Commission with the US Department of Justice (→ *9.10*). In 1998 it was, however, in substance, 're-concluded' by the Council as 'Agreement between the European Communities and the Government of the United

States of America regarding the application of their competition laws' and supplemented by the 'Agreement between the European Communities and the Government of the United States of America on the application of positive comity principles in the enforcement of their competition laws'.

11.5 Does the Community also possess implied powers to enter into international agreements?

As already noted, an express treaty-making competence of the EC was originally contained only in Articles 133 and 310 TEC with regard to the CCP and association agreements ($\rightarrow$ *11.1*). The elaboration of the **implied powers doctrine** ($\rightarrow$ *3.1*) in the area of external relations enabled the Community to enter into agreements in other fields where it had an **internal competence to legislate**. An apt description of this reasoning can be found in the ECJ's Opinion 2/91, *ILO Convention* [1993] ECR I-1061 where it is stated that:

> Authority to enter into international commitments may not only arise from an express attribution by the Treaty, but may also flow implicitly from its provisions . . .
> **whenever** Community law created for the institutions of the Community **powers** within its **internal system** for the purpose of attaining a specific objective, the Community had **authority** to **enter** into the **international commitments** necessary for the attainment of that objective even in the absence of an express provision in that connection.

11.6 Where did the ECJ find the Community's power to enter into international agreements according to the ERTA judgment?

The groundwork for such an extensive reading of the Community's external powers was laid in the Court's case law

of the early 1970s. In the so-called *ERTA* Case, Case 22/70
Commission v. *Council* [1971] ECR 263, the Court had to decide
whether the Commission (for the Community) or the Member
States (on their own behalf) had the competence to negotiate
a European Road Transport Agreement (ERTA) with third
countries.

The ECJ took as a starting point that Article 281 TEC
provided for the (international) **legal personality** of the
Community. It continued to reason that in order to establish
the Community's treaty-making power in a specific case it is
necessary to look at the **whole scheme** of the Treaty and not
only at single substantive provisions. The court then reaffirmed the implied powers doctrine by stating that the authority to enter into international agreements 'arises not only from
an express conferment by the Treaty but may equally flow
implicitly from other provisions of the Treaty, from the act of
accession and from measures adopted within the framework
of those provisions, by the Community institutions'. Finally,
the ECJ concluded that:

> each time the Community, with a view to implementing
> a common policy envisaged by the Treaty, adopts
> provisions laying down common rules, whatever form
> these may take, the Member States no longer have
> the right, acting individually or even collectively, to
> undertake obligations with third countries which affect
> those rules. As and when such common rules come into
> being, the Community alone is in a position to assume
> and carry out contractual obligations towards third
> countries affecting the whole sphere of application
> of the Community legal system. With regard to the
> implementation of the provisions of the Treaty the system
> of **internal Community** measures may **not** therefore be
> **separated** from that of **external relations**.

11.7 For its power to enter into agreements is it necessary that the EC has already exercised its internal legislative competence?

The *ERTA* Case seems to make exclusive **external powers dependent** upon the prior adoption of 'common rules', that is, Community legislation.

In the *Rhine Navigation* Case concerning a Draft Agreement Establishing a Laying-up Fund for Inland Waterway Vessels, Opinion 1/76 [1977] ECR 741, the Court clarified, however, that the EC was competent to enter into an agreement for the control of river traffic, although it had not yet exercised its internal competence to regulate inland waterway traffic based on its **power to regulate transport** 'insofar as the participation of the Community in the international agreement is, as here, necessary for the attainment of one of the objectives of the Community'. It is likely that the Court found an exclusive external competence of the Community in this very specialised field because it felt that individual Member State action could have threatened the common Community objective.

In later rulings the ECJ seemed to retreat from such broad assertions of Community powers.

In Opinion 1/94, *WTO Agreement* [1994] ECR I-5267 ($\rightarrow$ *11.10*), it made clear that external and internal powers are **not co-extensive** and that 'only insofar as common rules have been established at the internal level does the external competence of the Community become exclusive'.

? 11.8 Does the treaty-making power of the EC preclude the Member States from entering into agreements in the fields concerned?

In the case of an 'exclusive' Community competence, such as the CCP under Article 133 TEC, Member States have lost their power to enter into international agreements.

In the case of a 'concurrent' Community competence, however, this is different. In the *Kramer* Case, Joined Cases 3, 4 and 6/76 *Officier van Justitie* v. *Kramer and others* [1976] ECR 1279, Dutch rules on fish conservation according to the North-East Atlantic Fisheries Convention were upheld. The Court stated that 'it follows from the . . . duties and powers . . . on the internal level [fisheries are a common EC policy (→ *10.6*)] that the Community has authority to enter into international commitments for the conservation of [sea resources]'. However, 'the Community not yet having fully exercised its functions in the matter . . . the Member States had the power to assume commitments'. This concurrent authority of the Community's Member States is transitional, that is, valid until the EC resumes its authority, and limited by the Community principle of loyalty of Article 10 TEC which requires states to respect the common EC position.

? 11.9 Was the Community competent to conclude the International Rubber Agreement?

In addition to the complex issue of express and implied (external) powers of the Community (→ *11.2, 11.3, 11.5*), students of European law have to live with the notion that the treaty-making power of the EC does not always lie exclusively with the Community, but is more often shared with its Member States. In these cases of shared external competence, both the

Community and its Member States have to become parties to what is known in EC law as a 'mixed agreement'.

One of the leading cases in this field is the ECJ's Opinion 1/78 [1978] ECR 2817, on the procedure to be followed in order to enter into the International Rubber Agreement, which was negotiated under UNCTAD auspices as part of an Integrated Programme for Commodities. Commodity agreements aim at price and income stabilisation for developing countries. The Commission wanted to negotiate alone, claiming an exclusive Community competence under the Common Commercial Policy, while the Council recommended joint negotiations with the Member States because it regarded the agreement as a 'mixed' agreement.

The Court held that the agreement, 'a more structured instrument in the form of an organisation of the market', required direct financial contributions from the Member States and was thus 'characteristic of development aid'. As a result, it could **not** be **entirely based** on Article 133 TEC and, **therefore**, was to be concluded as a 'mixed agreement'.

> **?** **11.10 Who had the power to conclude the GATS and TRIPs Agreements resulting from the Uruguay Round negotiations?**

In 1994 the GATT Uruguay Round negotiations came to an end. The 1947 **General Agreement on Tariffs and Trade** (GATT), dealing with trade in goods, was incorporated largely unchanged into the GATT 1994. In addition, however, the Uruguay Round negotiations produced a new international organisation, the **World Trade Organization** (WTO), and resulted in numerous side agreements to the GATT, addressing matters such as anti-dumping, countervailing duties, etc., as well as two major treaties transcending strict trade in goods: the

1994 **General Agreement on Trade in Services** (GATS); and the 1994 **Agreement on Trade-Related Intellectual Property Rights** (TRIPs).

As a result of its exclusive competence in the field of external trade stemming from the Common Commercial Policy the EC had already taken over the external trade obligations of its Member States under the GATT well before the Uruguay Round, as the ECJ recognised in Case 21-24/72 *International Fruit Company* v. *Produktschap voor Groenten en Fruit* [1971] ECR 1219 (→ *4.12*), where it found that:

> insofar as under the EEC Treaty the Community has assumed the powers previously exercised by Member States in the area governed by the General Agreement, the provisions of that agreement have the effect of binding the Community.

In 1994, the fundamental issue arose whether the Community also had the **power** to **conclude** the **WTO** and the other **new agreements** on services and intellectual property. Again the ECJ's advice was sought. In Opinion 1/94, *WTO Agreement* [1994] ECR I-5267 (→ *11.7*), the Court held that only the **GATT** 1994, not **GATS** and **TRIPs** fell under the Community's exclusive competence. Thus, the latter two treaties had to be concluded as **'mixed agreements'**.

To understand the Court's reasoning one has to be aware of the GATS differentiation between different types of providing services according to four so-called **modes of supply**: cross-border, commercial presence or movement of either provider or consumer to the other WTO member. According to the ECJ, only **'cross-frontier supply'** situations were not unlike trade in goods and, thus, covered by Article 133 TEC (→ *11.2*), whereas **'consumption abroad'** and **'commercial presence'** – matters touching on such politically sensitive issues as entry rights for foreign nationals – related more to 'measures concerning the entry and movement of persons' where the Community did not have exclusive competence. Also with regard to TRIPs the ECJ adopted a middle way. It held that, with the exception of provisions concerning the prohibition of the release into free circulation of counterfeit goods ('measures to be taken by the customs authorities at the external frontiers of the Community'), TRIPs measures did not fall within the scope of the Community's CCP.

While the precise legal reasoning of the Court may sometimes be a little arcane, the outcome clearly reflects the political will of the Member States which had rejected proposals for a broad Community external economic policy competence suggested by the Commission during the Maastricht negotiations (→ 1.8).

One of the political consequences of Opinion 1/94 was the introduction of a new paragraph to Article 133 TEC during the Amsterdam Intergovernmental Conference. According to this new provision the Council may unanimously, after consulting the European Parliament, extend the scope of the Community's Common Commercial Policy to services and intellectual property. Since no action followed in the Council, the Nice Treaty has now written this extension of Community powers into the new paragraphs 5, 6 and 7 of Article 133 TEC. Both the Draft Constitution Treaty and the Lisbon Reform Treaty would have further broadened the external trade powers of the EC.

11.11 What is the legal basis for association agreements?

Article 310 TEC provides for the Community's power to enter into agreements establishing an association involving 'reciprocal

rights and obligations, common action and special procedures'. As a rule, association agreements are more than just
free trade agreements, often including rules on the free movement of persons, on investments, development aid, or other
economic issues. They regularly provide for special (legislative
and administrative) procedures and set up joint bodies, such as
Association Councils (→ *4.12*).

The first association agreement was concluded with Turkey
in 1963 in order to establish a customs union in three stages. It
moved on to the third stage in March 1995. In 1971 and 1973,
association agreements providing for two-stage customs unions
were concluded with Malta and Cyprus. So-called **cooperation
agreements**, legally also association agreements, were concluded with Mahgreb (Algeria, Tunisia, Morocco) and Mashrek
(Egypt, Jordan, Lebanon, Syria) states as well as with Israel and
the West Bank and Gaza Strip.

11.12 What is the significance of the Lomé Agreements?

Starting with the first **Yaoundé Agreement** in 1963 and followed by Yaoundé II in 1969, the EEC embarked on designing a web of cooperation agreements with the so-called **ACP**
(African, Caribbean and Pacific) countries, many of which
were former colonies of the EC Member States. Since 1975
relations between the ACP states and the Community have
been governed by the **Lomé Conventions**, which established a
far-reaching and complex partnership, focusing on economic
and development cooperation. Through a system of non-
reciprocal trade preferences certain manufactured and mostly
agricultural products (such as bananas, rice and sugar) entering
the Community were exempted from EC customs duties and
quantitative restrictions.

Lomé IV, the last Lomé Convention, was concluded in 1989 for a ten-year period. It emphasised development via self-reliant economies and sustainable development. It also introduced the promotion of human rights and respect for democracy as key elements of the partnership in so-called human rights conditionality clauses which have remained controversial politically. After the expiry of Lomé IV in 2000 ACP–EC relations were replaced by the **Cotonou Agreement**, which builds on the existing institutional and financial instruments of cooperation. Under the Cotonou Agreement, which has been concluded for a period of twenty years, the group of ACP countries has risen to seventy-seven.

11.13 Which other association agreements have been entered into by the Community?

The Community's enlargement process (→ *1.7*) was supported by the conclusion of so-called **Europe Agreements** with Eastern European countries in 1991 (Poland, Hungary and CSFR), 1993 (Czech Republic, Slovakia, Romania, Bulgaria) and 1995 (Estonia, Latvia, Lithuania). They aimed at establishing a free-trade area for industrial products by 2002 and preparing for accession by covering the main areas in which the *acquis communautaire* (→ *1.6*), was to be adopted.

Also, the EEA (**European Economic Area**) Agreement, concluded between the EC and the remaining individual EFTA countries (today Iceland, Liechtenstein and Norway, but not Switzerland which rejected EEA membership in a popular referendum), is an association agreement. The EEA basically extends all four freedoms and other Community policies and provides for a sophisticated institutional framework.

? 11.14 How did European political co-operation evolve?

The informal meetings of the **heads of state and government** of the EC Member States, today assembled in the 'European Council' (→ *2.2, 2.3*), starting with The Hague summit in 1969, led to a form of **political co-operation** which was first recognised in the 1986 SEA. It endorsed the foreign policy cooperation actually practised and provided in Article 30(1) that the Member States 'shall endeavour jointly to formulate and implement a European foreign policy' by 'informing and consulting each other'. A **political committee**, consisting of the political directors of the foreign ministries of the Member States, with its own secretariat in Brussels was formed. This Committee largely substitutes for COREPER (→ *2.8*) in preparing for European Council meetings.

The 1992 Maastricht Treaty formally established the **Common Foreign and Security Policy** (CFSP) with the following **objectives** laid down in Article J.1, now Article 11(1), TEU:

- to safeguard the **common values**, fundamental interests, independence and integrity of the Union in conformity with the principles of the United Nations Charter;
- to strengthen the **security** of the Union in all ways;
- to preserve **peace** and strengthen **international security**, in accordance with the principles of the United Nations Charter, as well as the principles of the Helsinki Final Act and the objectives of the Paris Charter, including those on external borders;
- to promote international **co-operation**; and
- to develop and consolidate **democracy** and the **rule of law**, and respect for **human rights** and fundamental freedoms.

? 11.15 How does the EU act in the second and third pillar?

The loose, intergovernmental form of co-operation in both the CFSP and PJCC ($\rightarrow$ 2.1) is reflected in the relatively weak instruments available to the EU when acting in these fields. The most important EU acts are as follows: According to Article 4 TEU the European Council defines the 'general political guidelines' of the Union. In the field of the CFSP, the European Council may then decide on 'common strategies' pursuant to Article 13 TEU, while the Council may adopt 'joint actions' (Article 15 TEU) or 'common positions' (Article 15 TEU) and conclude international agreements (Article 24 TEU).

In the justice and home affairs field, now PJCC, the Council may adopt 'common positions', 'framework decisions' (similar to directives in the first pillar) and 'decisions', or recommend the adoption of 'conventions', that is, international agreements, by the Member States (Article 34 TEU).

? 11.16 What is the role of the European Council in CFSP matters?

According to Article 13 TEU, the European Council 'defines the principles of and general guidelines for the common foreign and security policy, including for matters with defence implications'. Since the 1997 Amsterdam Treaty it also decides on 'common strategies to be implemented by the Union in areas where the Member States have important common interests'. Such 'common strategies' shall set out their objectives, duration and the means to be made available by the Union and the Member States. The first 'common strategy' was decided by the Cologne European Council in June 1999 and concerned the

Russian Federation. In 2000, common strategies were adopted for Ukraine and the Mediterranean region.

11.17 How do the EU Member States undertake 'joint actions'?

The CFSP is implemented by the Council of the EU, the foreign ministers in the General Affairs and External Relations Council ($\rightarrow$ 2.4), by means of common positions and joint actions. Article 14 TEU fixes the procedure for adopting joint actions which:

> address specific situations where operational action by the Union is deemed to be required. They shall lay down their objectives, scope, the means to be made available to the Union, if necessary their duration, and the conditions for their implementation.

The Council clearly has the decisive role. Although Member States and the Commission may make proposals, it is the Council which decides, on the basis of 'general guidelines' of the European Council ($\rightarrow$ 2.3, 11.16), whether there should be a 'joint action' at all and on the scope, objective and other issues. The first 'joint action' was the sending of election observers to Russia in December 1993. Many country-focused joint actions concerned the former Yugoslavia. Others address non-proliferation issues, in particular with respect to nuclear weapons, or bans on anti-personnel mines.

11.18 What other measures are taken in furtherance of the CFSP?

The Council also adopts 'common positions'. According to Article 15 TEU:

common positions shall define the **approach** of the Union
to a **particular matter** of a **geographical** or **thematic
nature**. Member States shall ensure that their national
policies conform to the common positions.

Not expressly mentioned in the TEU are **declarations** which
give public expression to a position, request or expectation of
the EU. This flexible instrument enables the EU to react very
quickly to international incidents and to state the Union's point
of view vis-à-vis a third country or any international question.
They are usually called 'Declarations by the European Union',
where the Council meets and adopts a position on an international issue and 'Declarations by the Presidency on behalf of
the European Union', where the Council does not meet. The EU
regularly issues more than a hundred declarations per year.

? 11.19 Why is the CFSP usually characterised as an intergovernmental form of cooperation?

Article 23(1) TEU confirms that, in principle, decisions on CFSP
matters are taken unanimously (→ 2.5). Though many CFSP
critics demand a departure from this form of intergovernmental
(unanimous) decision-making to supranational majority voting
for the sake of a more effective EU foreign policy, the unanimity principle has been only slightly modified. Article 23(2) TEU
permits **QMV** in cases of **implementing decisions**, such as
'adopting joint actions, common positions or taking any other
decision on the basis of a common strategy' or 'adopting any
decision implementing a joint action or a common position'. If,
however, 'a member of the Council declares that, for important
and stated reasons of national policy, it intends to oppose the
adoption of a decision to be taken by qualified majority' no vote
shall be taken and the matter will be referred to the **European
Council** for unanimous decision making. It is obvious that this

'procedural emergency brake' has been inspired by the 1966 Luxembourg Compromise.

A second modest erosion of the unanimity principle of Article 23 TEU can be found in its complex rules on **abstention**. Article 23(1), subparagraph 1 TEU clarifies that abstention does not prevent the adoption of a CFSP decision which is binding on all Member States. Article 23(1), subparagraph 2 TEU also introduced what has euphemistically been called a 'constructive abstention'. It provides that a Member State, when abstaining, 'may qualify its abstention by making a formal declaration'. This formal abstention implies that the abstaining Member State 'shall not be obliged to apply the decision, but shall accept that the decision commits the Union'. While the 'constructive' abstention leads to an effective opting-out, the abstaining Member State must 'refrain from any action likely to conflict with or impede Union action'. At the same time, the other EU Member States must respect the abstaining Member's position. If the combined weighted votes of Member States wishing to abstain under this provision represent one-third of the total votes, the 'constructive' abstention turns 'destructive' by preventing the adoption of a decision.

11.20 Does the EU have treaty-making power?

Article 24 TEU on the conclusion of international agreements in the field of the CFSP is an outstanding example of intentional ambiguity. On the one hand, it provides that agreements in the CFSP sphere are negotiated by the Presidency and 'concluded by the Council on a recommendation from the Presidency' – which indicates that these are EU treaties. On the other hand, it states that 'no agreement shall be binding on a Member State whose representative in the Council states that it has to comply with the requirements of its own constitutional procedure' – which may be taken to mean that these are, in fact, treaties concluded by the Council on behalf of the Member States. Apparently, the Member States could not agree on this issue and thus arrived at a compromise formulation which may be interpreted both ways.

? 11.21 Who is 'Mr CFSP' and what is the 'troika'?

Article 26 TEU provides that the Secretary-General of the Council ($\rightarrow$ 2.4) shall also be the High Representative for the Common Foreign and Security Policy, sometimes referred to as 'Mr CFSP'. According to this provision, introduced by the 1997 Amsterdam Treaty, the High Representative will assist the Council in CFSP matters by contributing in particular 'to the formulation, drawing up and implementation of political decisions and, when appropriate and acting on behalf of the Council at the request of the Presidency, through conducting political dialogue with third parties'. Pursuant to the wishes of the European Council, the High Representative should be 'a personality with a strong political profile', and in 1999 former NATO Secretary-General Javier Solana was appointed to this post. Mr CFSP is assisted by a 'Policy Planning and Early Warning Unit'.

The Amsterdam Treaty also changed the composition of the so-called 'troika', which is an informal Council formation representing the EC/EU in external affairs. Instead of the three Member States holding the actual, previous and following Presidency, the 'troika' now consists of the actual Presidency, the High Representative and the Commissioner for External Relations.

11.22 How does the EU/EC implement economic sanctions?

The adoption of economic sanctions against third states for political purposes provides a good example of the inter-relationship between the first and the second pillar, the supra-national law of the Community and the inter-governmental rules of the Union (→ *1.5, 2.7*). Since sanctions are of a hybrid nature – they are economic measures for political goals – both the TEC's Common Commercial Policy and the TEU's CFSP are potentially relevant.

In practice, the Treaties have codified a compromise procedure already developed under the European Political Cooperation (→ *1.8, 11.14*). First, a CFSP 'common position' or 'joint action' is adopted (→ *11.17, 11.18*). Then, according to Article 301 TEC, the Council, by a qualified majority on a proposal from the Commission, takes the 'necessary urgent measures', usually regulations aimed at banning imports and/ or exports from the targeted countries (→ *3.8*).

11.23 Does the EU possess a European security and defence policy?

According to Article 17(1) TEU, the 'common foreign and security policy shall include all questions relating to the security of the Union, including the progressive framing of a common defence policy, which might lead to a common defence, should the European Council so decide'. This provision is the core of a still infant European Security and Defence Policy (ESDP), which is in constant danger of being marginalised by NATO, on the one hand, and by being effectively 'neutralised' by the interests of neutral Member States, on the other hand. The latter interests are protected by the rather cryptic 'Irish' clause of Article 17(1) TEU, according to which, the ESDP 'shall not prejudice the specific character of the security and defence policy of certain Member States'.

The Amsterdam Treaty provides that ESDP includes the so-called **Petersberg tasks**, that is, 'humanitarian and rescue tasks, **peace-keeping** tasks and tasks of combat forces in **crisis management**, including peacemaking'. In 2003, the first ESDP missions took place on the basis of unanimously approved joint actions, among them the European Police Mission in Bosnia and Herzegovina, 'Operation Concordia' in the Former Yugoslav Republic of Macedonia and 'Operation Artemis', the first EU peace-keeping mission outside Europe, in the Democratic Republic of the Congo.

11.24 Who pays for CFSP and ESDP?

According to Article 18 TEU, **administrative expenditure** is charged to the **budget** of the **EC**. Since the 1997 Amsterdam Treaty, the same applies in principle to **operational expenditure**. However, operational expenditure 'arising from operations having military or defence implications', that is, **ESDP** costs, are borne by the **Member States** 'in accordance with the gross national product scale'. Member States having exercised their right to 'constructive abstention' ($\rightarrow$ *11.19*) are exempted from contributing.

Index